Hard

Pieces

Hard
Pieces

Dan Carpenter's Indiana

Dan Carpenter

Edited by David Hoppe

Indiana University Press

BLOOMINGTON AND INDIANAPOLIS

The paper used in this publication meets the minimum requirements of American National Standard for Information Sciences—Permanence of Paper for Printed Library Materials, ANSI Z39.48-1984.

MANUFACTURED IN THE UNITED STATES OF AMERICA

Library of Congress Cataloging-in-Publication Data

Carpenter, Dan, date
    Hard pieces : Dan Carpenter's Indiana / Dan Carpenter ; edited by David Hoppe.
      p. cm.
    ISBN 0-253-31316-3 (cloth). — ISBN 0-253-31317-1 (pbk.)
    1. Indiana—Social life and customs.   I. Hoppe, David, date.
II. Title
F526.6.C37   1993
977.2—dc20   93-9960

1 2 3 4 5 97 96 95 94 93

For Mary, Patrick, and Erin Carpenter

CONTENTS

Dan Carpenter is a Midwestern writer. He has lived in Indianapolis most of his life; he works for *The Indianapolis Star* newspaper. Dan wrote the pieces collected in this book for *The Star* over the course of approximately 10 years. You might say that these pieces are "about" people and places in Indiana. That would be true, of course. This book is full of the faces, gestures, and voices of people making lives for themselves during a particular period in a particular place. But what I find most compelling here is the point of view of the writer who has identified these stories and the straightforward way in which he tells them. I think it is a distinctively Midwestern way—and I believe it is worth attending to.

Calling someone like Dan Carpenter a Midwestern writer is not an uncomplicated thing to do. Regionalism and the labels that go with it can be a trick bag of cliché, stereotype, parochialism, and mediocrity. It takes a genuine sensibility, a truly distinctive voice to achieve real authenticity. More is at stake here than simply rendering descriptions of people and places with verisimilitude. One seeks a deeper connection to the material, an ethic or vision that seems inevitably wedded to the sense of place. This collection demonstrates that Dan Carpenter brings such a sense of place to his writing. It is an encouraging discovery.

For all our party-line hyperbole about hometown values and down-to-earth practicality, a close look indicates that we Midwesterners really don't love ourselves that much. What we like to call modesty is actually a kind of collective low self-esteem. How else does one account for the fact that our region's cultural history is, in large part, the story of the flight of its most talented people? Or that a reading of our landscape—rural and urban—is so consistently about the triumph of short-term economic gain over longer-term communal and environmental values?

As we approach the psychic quake of a new millennium, there are those among us who, in radio-voice tones, would have us believe that the Midwest is the last place in America where things somehow stay a mythical "same." This, in spite of usurpation of family farms by corporate powers, the erosion of small-town viability, unchecked suburban sprawl around our cities, and the promiscuous use of undeveloped lands for anything from out-of-state waste dumps to amusement parks.

Things in the Midwest have been—and are—changing. Which makes it like the rest of the United States. But the Midwest has lacked advocates. We haven't New England's old school tie nostalgia or the Pacific Coast's grommet-eyed optimism; the Old South's Gothic appreciation for intersections of pleasure and pain or the West's cult of violent individualism. Our landscape, lacking the obvious drama afforded by mountains or oceanside, is an acquired taste.

Unlike these other places, where local mythologies seem almost pre-packaged, Midwestern stories are rarely told—and when they are, too often, the telling is in the service of sentimentality that seeks not to make sense of things but to avoid them. The national media turn the Midwest into a backdrop for enactments of simple virtues, homely eccentricity or the inbred exoticism of truly aberrant behavior. Unfortunately, many of us play along, mistaking stereotyping for validation.

But with everything else, this too may be changing. Which is where Dan Carpenter and the stories he tells come in.

First, I believe Dan Carpenter is one person who does love it here. His personal history and the history of this place are intertwined. This makes it extremely difficult—if he is to write well—for him to use clichés where honesty is in order or to nod and say "progress" when he witnesses the buildings, landscape, or people he associates with the heritage of this place being demolished or forgotten.

Dan has written that his primary interest has been with the stories of people living on the margins of society. This collection bears that out. What is striking is that he has chosen his subjects not to advance an ideological agenda but as a way of defining what, for him, the hallmarks of community in Indiana have been about and to illuminate what is being lost during this endlessly "transitional" time. The point being that not all these losses are necessary. We have choices, just as Dan has chosen to write these stories; thereby, in his way, paying homage to the subjects that make them possible.

And, as he has chosen to stay and make his writing life in Indiana.

I said that this is encouraging because for most of this century Midwestern writers, from Fitzgerald and Hemingway to Kurt Vonnegut, have written as exiles. American prose has gained, perhaps even been defined, by their combined contribution. The Midwest, on the other hand, has never developed a literature of place and, by extension, a self-definition comparable to the well-published East, South, or, more recently, West. Dan Carpenter's writing makes it clear that our heritage is more vulnerable for this; for stories are the stuff of memory and where memories are dim or given to the conveniences of soft sentiment, there is no end to the mischief that people may do. It also suggests a range of possibilities, the extent of work yet to be done.

If a writer of vignettes—word pictures—spends his days in quest of the perfect scene, then my stint with *The Indianapolis Star* reached its summit a few days after Thanksgiving of 1990, in a crowded mortuary in Paoli, Indiana.

The funeral of Lotus Dickey, a sublime and devout septuagenarian fiddle player who'd lived in a log cabin in the Orange County hills, was where I was headed when I'd begun scrawling in the margins of Indiana life more than a decade earlier.

Filled with gospel music, tears, and stories, virtually devoid of fashion content, the event was, as I described it in my column a few days later, "one of those flower-perfect moments of grace that life offers up to redeem all its strife and stinginess."

The sorrow in that blessing was hard-earned. From my angle of vision, the 1980s were a period of enormous stress upon the human and wild communities, a time of technology and acquisitiveness run rampant, a long siege against tradition and integrity and beauty.

Many of the more than 1,500 columns I wrote during those years were angry polemics, on the strength of which I was neatly labeled the house liberal and subjected to reviews of my work in the letters-to-the-editor column.

More interesting than my opinions, I thought, were the people I chased with my notebook, through whose lives I was able to celebrate or at least test my ideals of persistence, fidelity, diversity, imagination—all the best excuses for reading and writing stories, fact and fiction.

Often I found my stories lying in full view of the rest of journalism, like gold nuggets on an island of barterers. Who but I cared that W. W. Wilno, then a sickly man in his 70s, once a world-famous daredevil thrust 60 feet into the air every night by a cannon of his own manufacture, was quietly training teenage circus performers in Peru, Indiana, in the 1980s? Who else wanted The Great Wilno, Human Cannonball of the Jazz Age, when he was giving his final history lesson? "Just keep my name going," he said as we parted, and that still seems a decent ambition for me.

Like one of my favorite writers, Edward Hoagland, I've been a sucker for the circus because it's so flamboyantly out of synch and so unabashed about overstaying its welcome in these days past wonder. The golden animal trainer Gunther Gebel-Williams drew my pursuit less because he was the trade's biggest star than because he reminded me of the Amishman, the peace activist, the minor league baseball player. He was, like so many of my subjects of far less prominence, an anachronism that refused to be a relic—the soul of relevance, the very salt of the times.

"I don't need a great yuppie lifestyle," a young throwback named Anne Farringer told me after a cold October afternoon working as a nurse to the homeless. "I'm like the people on the street, who just want to have dignity, some friendships, a chance to go your way." Add those words to the image of her and one of her patients, a fellow in a downtown park who carries a bullet wound in his leg from a big-city argument and the nickname Angel of Death from Vietnam, and you have the equivalent of at least a dozen editorials.

Pictures preach powerfully. It seemed as if everything I'd learned on this wonderful beat in this grinding decade was captured in the Kanakaria mosaics, chunks of religious art from sixth-century Cyprus that became war booty, then black market commodities, then the prize in an Indianapolis court battle covered by *The New York Times* itself. In 1991, two years after the trial, I finally saw them displayed:

"Jagged, dulled and chipped, the four faces that looked back at me radiated a calm and a wholeness that mocked all the strife they had survived. They reminded me of some people I've known, who gained a little fame for one reason or another and found it funny because they actually deserved it."

I present this collection as a partial mosaic of contemporary Indiana, rural and urban and—whenever I could help it—on the edge. The articles that made the cut are not regional in any premeditated or niche-seeking way; yet it seems impossible to appreciate the country fiddler, the retired human cannonball, the inner-city preacher, or the rest of this tableau outside their time and place. I have assembled their group portrait in the spirit of preservation, and each of its glass fragments continues to hold light for me. May some of them reflect to others the grace I've known in their making.

The articles herein were published originally in *The Indianapolis Star*, some in slightly different form. My thanks to superiors and colleagues who indulged my writing them, helped make them better, and labored with me to prepare them for new publication.

Crossroads
and
Cul-de-Sacs

Sleeping Safe

Cairo, Ind.—There is no sign identifying this place, and not much place to identify, really. Just an intersection of county roads a few miles north of Lafayette, framed by two houses and two muddy fields.

One of those houses used to be the general store, Cairo's only business, closed more than 30 years. In the conversion, they left the cement stoop and its crowd of ghosts from a once-lively trade.

The storefront won't stop traffic any more, but another relic will. In a windswept lot behind the building, along the gravel County Road 850 North, across from the junk-strewn yard of a mobile home, stands a sight in defiance of time.

First, there's the tower. Thirty-two feet high, set on four utility poles, a skeleton of peeling timbers and barely readable signs. "Tower closed for repairs, no trespassing beyond gate," one sign says. But the lowest section of stairs has been removed anyway to keep the kids out, as has the little wood hut that used to occupy the top.

A few yards away, there's the monument. Fifteen feet high, 10 tons-plus of Indiana limestone. A statue of a man, woman, and boy, looking skyward, crowns a massive base on which is inscribed "1976—They Also Serve Who Stand And Watch."

This is Post Delta Lima 3 Green, one of 20,000 civilian volunteer lookout stations in the U.S. Air Force Ground Observer Corps, a Cold War vigilance program that started in 1952 and lasted two years in Cairo and eight years nationally.

The remnants are here mostly because of a 69-year-old man named Lawrence W. O'Connor, who wants them to serve "as a reminder to people, a reminder to young people, that their predecessors cared about their country."

Tiny Cairo cared enough to build a tower, whereas most of the 2.5 million Americans who scanned the skies for Soviet planes in those days did so from porches, yards and rooftops. And Cairo (say it "Karo") had the first observer post to be commissioned by the Air Force.

The late Charles A. Halleck, then the 2nd District congressman, was there for that ceremony on Aug. 16, 1952. The term "Those who stand and watch" was his.

O'Connor also was there. He ran the general store that closed in 1957, and still lives with his wife, Nora, in the house that absorbed the store. Their eight children shared the back yard with Post Delta Lima 3 Green.

At the request of then-Gov. George N. Craig, O'Connor was the post supervisor. He commanded a skywatching effort that enlisted more than 100 citizens—five times Cairo's immediate population—and kept the tower occupied around the clock for better than a year.

It was O'Connor's idea to have the monument carved in conjunction with the Bicentennial in 1976. He and a small band of friends finally brought it to Cairo for dedication—four years later—by paying off a debt of several thousand dollars (he won't say exactly how much) to the Bedford company that made it.

"Some people thought we were crazy, putting in that time and everything," O'Connor says. "But I was an ex-serviceman. I'd been in the war. All this red-herring stuff—there were threats back then. . . . As for me, anything Uncle Sam asked me, I would do my best. Others around here felt the same way."

Officially, civilian ground observers were a backup against the evasion or disruption of the military's electronic surveillance by hostile aircraft. Halleck thundered in his speech about rumored Soviet radar-cheating bombers. Volunteers in Cairo didn't spot any Soviet planes, but their duty was to log every plane they did see and phone in an "Aircraft Flash." They were awarded little silver wing pins and were supplied with distance charts and silhouettes of American, British, and Soviet aircraft.

"People would sit up there and imagine they saw flying saucers, UFOs," O'Connor says with a chuckle. "You get up there in those stars and you're like to see anything. But hell, they're still reporting UFOs today.

"We had romance happen up there. Young guy and gal stood watch together and they got married."

The memories fill his head and several boxes. They hang from a wall and blare from audiotapes. There's a letter from President Ford, a stack of signed loyalty oaths, a newspaper photo of "me, hamming it up for the camera." There's a creased poster showing a child with a teddy bear—"SAFE Because YOU Watch the Skies."

Outside, where politicians and marching bands boomed forth in 1952 and 1980, Post Delta Lima 3 Green is alone with the clang of its wind-whipped flagpole and the cry of a scavenging phoebe. O'Connor hopes to get a plaque put up there some day. But for now, the few passers-by who pause get the story from a cracked piece of plywood on which the former commander has hand-lettered his own tribute to "the many thousands of U.S. citizens who volunteered their services and resources in the defense of our country."

They Who Stand and Wait

She's like a lot of women in the ruined rural neighborhood that the social scientists call Appalachia. She has made her life without a man—and in spite of one.

Counselors told her it was just like combat fatigue, that dazed and frightened aspect she took on after years with a mean drunk husband. By the time she broke free of him, she had brought two beautiful children into their 20s with high school diplomas and absolute devotion to her.

Finding work was easy where they lived, depending how you looked at it. Pizza Hut and McDonald's were usually hiring. If you wanted to do better, you could hope the Japanese built another factory nearby. Or you could move to a city. Sitting on the hood of a car in a Harley-Davidson T-shirt, drinking beer with your buddies, was sort of a regional vocation.

Sister did the McDonald's thing, got married, and kept her sights on college or business school. Brother made a decision. Leaving his pals to nurse their beat-up cars and their traffic court cases, he joined the Navy.

His mother held her heart with both hands. She believed as strongly as he that he had to get out of there. She was proud to see his initiative. But it had been half a lifetime since she had lived without him. Young as she had been when her children were born, she was as much sister to them as mother. To have him reduced to a white-hatted portrait on the wall and a hollow voice on the phone was like an amputation.

She could laugh about her suffering, though. It was just for a few years, after all. There were calls and letters and furloughs to anticipate.

And he loved it. He made petty officer rapidly, won commendations, described to her in a deepened voice how he trained other sailors. She meant it when she said "I miss him to death," but she was chiding herself too.

It grieved him that he couldn't go home to see his sister get married, but duty was his solace and his phone call was theirs. He sounded so wonderful, his man's voice bridging a thousand miles that wedding night, stern and confident and happy.

Over the ensuing months, the war and his sister's baby approached together. The petty officer waited on the East Coast for important old men to send him to the Persian Gulf. In the small town he had escaped, his young mother awaited her first grandchild and his calls, hoping the protective shell she had formed in her brutal marriage would hold.

The little girl came early, but the labor was long. The expectant mother and dad, another good young man with staying power, spent all of a Sunday in the hospital with the expectant grandmother.

The sailor called three times. He told his mother not to worry. He told her forms had been passed out on which each man wrote his will. The television stayed tuned to CNN, reinforcing the terrifying futility of two men with armies playing chicken.

When the baby came the following evening, her exhausted parents and grandmother wept and giggled and marveled at her black curls. Grandma went to the phone to call the new uncle. She reached a recording. He had shipped out, it said, and all civilian communication was cut off for security reasons. Saddam Hussein's deadline was hours away.

The young grandmother went home and cried for many hours. When she returned to the hospital, the new baby, bathed and buffed, was even more beautiful than when she'd left her.

"And you know I wouldn't brag," she said.

Sure, came the reply. And seriously, maybe the timing was meant to be. Maybe this rosy little kid is an omen.

"That's what I'm hoping," she said.

Woods Wisdom

French Lick, Ind. — Banks McBride walks as he speaks and speaks as he walks, at a pace and pitch that force the newer world to slow down or lose out.

Smiling and steady, he hikes the rugged woods of Tillery Hill next to Patoka Lake, barely within earshot of three men up ahead who are three decades younger.

"Sunflowers," he'll say, no louder than he would if they were right beside him. "There's a nice poplar. Nice white oak, too."

His companions, two of them neighbors, interrupt their discussion of heavy-duty environmental issues to share his intimacy with this spindly woods that used to be grudging farmland.

"Not far from here, they used to roll logs into the river and raft 'em down to Jasper," the quiet man in the Big Mac bib overalls points out. "The river was so crooked, they could have lunch and dinner at the same farmhouse."

The crooked Patoka River is now the sprawling Patoka Lake, of course. The land on which Banks McBride and his friends stand is owned by the federal government and leased to the state government, which in turn plans to lease it to businessmen to build an $80-million resort.

While the pros and cons of that proposal are being debated and battles over environmental impact and master plans and such are being waged, Banks McBride is in the forest, on this November day in 1988, seeing trees.

His friends love the woods, too. They chose to live here, attracted by the very lack of development from which the business-

men and government propose to rescue southern Indiana. Mc-
Bride was born in the area 72 years ago and still lives on his farm
in Cuzco, though he rents out the fields now.

The difference between McBride and his friends is that they
are bilingual—they talk political as well as plain, depending on
the occasion. His language is solely of his time and place, and it
and they are in peril.

A lot of people of his generation aren't on farms down here
any more because they sold out to the government under eminent domain—at prices many called ripoffs—when the lake was
created in the 1960s and 1970s.

"Some of them didn't want to move out," Banks McBride observes, "but I guess they had to."

They had to move for the cause of economic development,
the same cause behind the proposed resort. There's no question
the area is poor; and no question a lot of local people back the
project and wish the tree-huggers would shut up.

Reita Noble, a lifelong resident of Orange County who lives
on a 77-acre farm nearby, put it this way on a drive over to Tillery
Hill in her Volkswagen Rabbit:

"A yuppie friend of mine said, 'The only people at that meeting [last July] who objected were women who needed to shave
their legs.' She said, 'Reita, your property would be worth
$245,000.' I said, 'My property is not for sale.' That's the bottom
line—greed."

If they build this resort, they'll need new roads to draw in still
more city tourists. There's a good chance an access road would
run fairly close by Banks McBride's farm. You don't have to ask
him what he thinks of that idea.

It's not that nobody has asked him; but on the other hand, it's
not as though the world is slowing down to listen very well to an old
farmer who picks his lunch off a persimmon tree smack on top of a
future golf course. As for Banks, he's seen enough of the future.

"When they built the lake," he says, "they brought in a lot of
people that had to keep their houses locked."

Free Wheeling

Harrodsburg, Ind.—The majestic blue-and-white bookmobile has just lumbered over the hill from Old Ind. 37 and eased into its gravel parking space in the middle of town when Lee Maines pulls up in her rusty green 15-year-old Chevy.

Laboriously, her legs held in braces, the tall gray-haired lady steps aboard into a miniature library of light wood paneling, tilted shelves, air-conditioning, and neatly classified inventory.

New Fiction. Westerns. Reserve Books. Juvenile Non-Fiction.

Records from KISS to the soundtrack from *Mary Poppins*.

Magazines, from *Newsweek* to *National Geographic* to *Rolling Stone*.

Lee Maines grabs a 10-book stack of Nancy Drew and the Hardy Boys—"They're good when you don't want to get too involved"—and asks if anyone knows how the mushroom hunting is going.

Tami Shields, the high school student who runs the L-shaped checkout desk near the driver's seat, replies that her parents found some the other day.

A few more seconds of chatter about mushrooms and books, and Lee Maines is out the padded door, to be followed over the next two hours by several dozen readers, browsers, picture-lovers, and writers of school papers, ranging in age from about 3 to 60.

"I live by myself. I'm lonesome. I enjoy reading," Ms. Maines tells the man from the newspaper. "I also write a lot of letters, and I get information out of my books and pass it on."

If the bookmobile did not make its regular Tuesday night stops in her southern Indiana town of 350 people, Lee Maines would have to drive 10 miles to the Monroe County Public Library in Bloomington. That would be hard on her and hard on her car; and besides, she's never written a poem about the Monroe County Public Library, only about its bookmobile.

> This truck is driven by a nice young man
> With a smile upon his face . . .

"It's interesting," says the nice young man, whose name is Walt Owens. "Some people prefer to use the bookmobile. Maybe it's less intimidating than the library. You don't have to go upstairs to find the children's section, for instance; you just turn around. It's more personal. I don't have as many patrons, and most of them know me."

The bearded, bespectacled, mellow-voiced Owens has been Monroe County's bookmobile librarian less than a year, wheeling the $50,000 Barth vehicle to Bloomington suburbs and remote rural communities such as Harrodsburg, Unionville, Smithville, Kirksville, Stanford, Dolan, and Clear Creek.

"This is a contact point for them between where they are and the larger society," Owens says. "The service we give—if it weren't for that, there would be none at all."

Common in Kentucky, Ohio, and other states, rural bookmobiles are a rarity in Indiana. Among the factors that make bookmobiles feasible is a combination of isolation and concentration—having people far enough from urban areas to need the service, and numerous enough to justify the staff and fuel to reach them.

Harrodsburg is a good stop. On the average, Owens says, 100 to 150 volumes are checked out of the van, which parks two doors down from the one-room post office and a half-mile from the town's wooden-floored gasoline station.

When things are slow, Tami catches up on her homework and Walt sips coffee from a thermal jug and arranges returned books in a large canvas bag. He won't be able to record the returns and borrowings until he gets back to home base; but a grant is being sought for an on-board computer that would link him and his patrons directly to the main building.

In the meantime, Owens keeps a pretty fair handle on his 3,000 volumes in his head. Without missing a beat, he can point this lady to Danielle Steel, this man to Stephen King, that teenager to cookbooks, and that pre-teen to books on karate.

"Someone may be going to have open-heart surgery, and I can find a book on it for them," he says. "Or someone may want a book on auto repair and I might have it. There's a lot of satisfaction in that."

With nightfall, the Harrodsburg connection is broken for another week. Like a solitary ocean liner with its banks of orange safety lights, the mammoth van heaves away from the corner of Gore Street and Popcorn Road, headed north. Two nights hence, Walt Owens will be Unionville's smiling librarian.

Bringing It Home

Washington, Ind. — They might have come from entirely different worlds, these two men who faced each other across a table in a back room of the Daviess County Courthouse on a sunny spring afternoon in 1989.

Over here, Bill Breeden, wearing an Army surplus fatigue shirt, his gaunt, goateed face framed by a ponytail and a bandana, his liberty on the line because of a political prank.

Over there, Richard Poindexter, neat and ample in his black sport coat, gray hair razor-cut to just over the top of the ear, Republican blood boiling over left-wing lawlessness.

Breeden, who lives in the woods in a teepee. Poindexter, who bears the biggest name in the little town of Odon and used to have a cousin in the White House.

Poles apart, they seemed. But that's just the problem. They are far from strangers. Their families go back generations together, and their closeness has infused a legally trivial court case with a passion that hurts.

"I was disappointed in Bill more than anything else," Poindexter said as he gave his pretrial deposition to Breeden's lawyers. "I've known him since he was a little boy. There was been nothing between the families but love and understanding. I wouldn't steel a 'Breeden' street sign."

Breeden awaits trial on charges of stealing an Odon street sign honoring Adm. John M. Poindexter, the native son who resigned as President Reagan's national security adviser because of the Iran-Contra scandal.

Breeden insists it was nothing personal. It just seemed wrong to enshrine a name associated with government deceit and the fomenting of civil war in other countries.

To Dick Poindexter, all was innocence till Bill came along. The erection of the street sign was a nonpolitical tribute to a bright boy who had once sold popcorn at the local bijou and had gone on to achieve the Navy's highest rank.

When Poindexter saw the newspaper photograph of Breeden displaying the missing sign with his cousin's name on it, he was good and mad. He could not understand "breaking the law to further your ideological aims—especially in a Christian community."

Especially by a minister, which Breeden is. Especially after all the families have been through together.

Poindexter, proprietor of Odon's only funeral home, buried Breeden's father and probably will bury his ailing mother. When Breeden's brother, George, was injured fatally in a farm accident, Poindexter came out with the ambulance.

How in the world, Poindexter pleaded, could a member of this God-fearing family and community do something as "idiotic" as smearing Odon's name and helping the communist Sandinistas in Nicaragua?

Breeden sat calmly through all this; but afterward, he flashed some passion of his own.

He said his family has given sons to the military since the War for Independence. One of them was his late brother, George, who did two tours in Vietnam. "They didn't fight," he snapped, "for what we've got now."

The pacifist proposes to argue that point with a jury of his small-town peers, even if the state insists this is not a political matter.

"It would have been easy to go to Washington, D.C., and protest and spend five days in prison," Breeden said. "Doing it here is a lot more difficult, but it's also a lot more educational. This forces them to grapple with what I do and why I do it. There's a lot of pain for me and for them; and I feel for them."

Coyote-Calling

Mitchell, Ind.—The portable broadcast speaker points westward from the hood of Larry Lehman's state-owned pickup truck, hurling its banshee voice toward a stand of trees backlit by the setting sun.

The answer, however, comes from the east, just beyond a pasture where three indifferent cows graze. Nothing new to people here in rural southern Indiana—and nothing pretty to some farmers—the sound still has a lonesome, haunted beauty, delicate as the air.

Lehman hears it instantly. "There you go," he says, his baked outdoorsman's face bursting into a smile.

In the space of a few seconds, the long, pure "o-o-o-o-o" pauses, rises again, then descends into a series of rapid rascally yips. Two, three more times, in different cadences, the sequence repeats. Then the cry of the coyote is gone, the breeze and bird-calls seamlessly refilling the space it has left.

"If in late July or early August you play these tapes and get no response, you can pretty well conclude there are no coyotes in the area," Lehman says during the drive to another back country spot. "The difficulty, however, is in determining how many there are when you've found them."

There were a great many more after the 1970s than after the 1960s. That was why Lehman began trying to keep track of them in the early 1980s in his capacity as fur-bearer research biologist for the Fish and Wildlife Division of the Indiana Department of Natural Resources.

On this cool spring evening, he is demonstrating the method

used in a recent field study, in which tapes of coyote howls, police sirens, and train whistles were played to elicit responses from *Canis iatrans.* The overall response rate was 6 percent, but the rate at peak season—late summer—was more than 20 percent.

What does it mean? It doesn't mean Lehman knows yet how many coyotes are in Indiana (he estimates 10,000 to 20,000). It doesn't mean he knows yet why they increased geometrically in the 1970s or why they leveled off in the 1980s. Much more field research is needed, and unfortunately Lehman cannot get the necessary time away from his desk these days. In wildlife research and management, the state's priority is the mushrooming deer population.

Predation by deer is an undisputed problem for Indiana farmers. Coyote damage to livestock is serious in some southern and western pockets of the state, but Lehman's questionnaires, calls, and letters tell him the overall harm from coyotes is no greater than that from free-running dogs. He also suggests that coyotes, which feed on rodents, can benefit farmers.

"No wildlife is all black or all white. There are problems with all of them," he says, steering down another rutted road as darkness falls. "I am willing to pay the price of some problems for the sake of variety."

He picks and chooses his words, recalling ruefully the flak he caught from people who got the impression from past newspaper articles that he places "his" coyotes above domestic animals.

"Maybe as a biologist I should be detached and not interested," he says, "but I do think that as long as you don't have too many problems or too great an impact on husbandry, it's a neat animal."

Suddenly, he breaks off and cocks his head toward the west. "I think I do hear one off that way," he says. But if it was a coyote cry, competing with the farm hounds and the frantic whippoorwills, it is gone.

"They're an interesting animal," Lehman says, "and a lot remains to be learned about them."

Rail Rider

Noblesville, Ind. —The wood fire under Snapshot's chili spewed its acrid, palpable smoke—the kind that hangs from the roof of your mouth for days—through the temporary hobo jungle in lovely, aptly named Forest Park.

Snapshot didn't seem to mind the tear-jerking fumes or the gnats that swarmed around him and his chopped peppers and onions and his hissing skillet of ground beef. To Snapshot, who gives his real name as Michael Carey, dinner duty under the stars beats room service at the Radisson. Not that he recommends the hobo life to anybody else.

"It's glamorous only in retrospect," he said, so glib and mellow he could pass as a late-night FM disc jockey. "It's hungry. It's extremely tiring. It's dangerous. The old-timers—how can I put this?—have a tendency to kind of embellish their stories. From my standpoint, it's not necessary. So many things actually happen that no one would believe anyway. You tend to forget the bad and remember the beauty."

Snapshot is a genuine hobo, just like Gas Can Paddy walking his dog over by the boxcars and A Man Called John telling stories about his water-witching powers at the picnic table. But Snapshot is a new hobo, if you will, and he looks new. He wears jeans with most of the blue still in them, a scarlet flannel shirt that could have come from the L. L. Bean catalog, and a rakish blue beret with a Nickel Plate Railroad pin affixed. His gray beard is trimmed, not spilling over his shirt like Paddy's or John's or Steam Train Maury's.

Snapshot (he likes to take pictures) is 42, a generation younger than those men; but he rides more freights than they do these days. He and his wife, Sylvia, live in the Florida Panhandle in winter, picking fruit and planting trees and such for their income, eschewing electricity, doing their washing and drinking in the creek. When it's warm to the north, Snapshot travels—by hitchhiking and boxcar, usually. When he's in a hurry, he's not too proud to fly.

Last year, Snapshot said, he rode freights five days to make the national hobo convention in Britt, Iowa. Last Friday, he took a Super Saver to reach Hobo Days, the weekend celebration hosted by the Indiana Transportation Museum, whose restored depot office and long lines of rail cars and engines are at the edge of Forest Park.

Snapshot flew, he said, because that meant he could postpone quitting his latest job five days. The common denominator about hobos is that they work for their freedom. They won't be classified with bums or tramps, seeking handouts.

"How one gets started—that takes a lot of reflection," Snapshot replied to a typical question. He traced his story back 39 years ago to West Bend, Wisconsin, when he was visiting his wealthy grandparents and a traveling man came to the door of their house on the hill.

"My grandmother gave him a bag of food. Whether I said at that time, 'This is what I want to do,' I must have always been a free spirit."

He's a free spirit who's managed to get in 15 years of formal schooling, by his account. He plans to go back to school and study computers, for heaven's sake. He could saddle up to the economy of mortgages and Blue Cross any time, as some of the old-timers have done in grudging deference to their aching knees.

But that's tomorrow. He might "catch a westbound" by then—that's hobo language for dying. Tonight, under the trees, he's the cook.

"You make pretty good chili," somebody said.

"I'd make chateaubriand if you'd bring me a tenderloin," Snapshot the hobo replied.

Bluegrass Mecca

Beanblossom, Ind. — Around one more bend of meandering old Ind. 135, some 40 miles and some considerable years from the big city, you happen upon one of those little billboards on wheels at the edge of a pasture.

In commercially quaint Brown County, the flashing yellow sign could be hawking hand-turned coffee mugs or fresh strawberries. When you read BILL MONROE'S BIGGEST BLUEGRASS FESTIVAL IN USA, you might wonder if some country folks are pulling your leg.

That's unless you know what you're looking for. In 1985, his 19th year of hosting a spring extravaganza of traditional hill music on the 96-acre farm he owns in absentia, Bill Monroe has nigh on no need for advertising.

By the thousands, in vans and pickup trucks and Hondas, from Arkansas and California and Wisconsin, with highbrow novels and copies of the *National Enquirer* to pass the time between shows, bluegrass lovers and bluegrass players find their way to this homely wooded Mecca.

Their stars — the Bill Monroes and Ralph Stanleys and Jimmy Martins — may be unknowns to the average fan of Bruce Springsteen or Wayne Newton. That's just fine. You don't take the grandkids along to Las Vegas and you don't bring your camper to Market Square Arena and hunker down for three or five or 10 days, sampling the music when you please.

"It's a purer form of country music and it's family-oriented," Talmadge Law said Friday after his band, Talmadge Law and the

Bluegrass Sounds, opened the 10-day gathering. "Bluegrass people are close-knit. You'd find you really have a mixture of different backgrounds but we all share a common bond."

Law, who is from the Trafalgar area, practices what he preaches. The band in which he plays fiddle and sings is all family—wife Betty on bass; son Aaron on mandolin; son Tom (only 15) on banjo; and son-in-law Brian Sawyer on guitar.

An automotive engineer who still carries the accent of his native Kentucky, Law decided long ago that bluegrass would have to be a weekend hobby, not a career. Though they play professionally, it is easy for the Laws to feel kinship with the many guitar-carrying and fiddle-toting people in their audience—"parking lot pickers," they call them at Beanblossom.

Friday's scene was especially intimate because the thousands weren't here yet. Only dozens had braved the overcast skies and sticky mud to hear the lesser lights of bluegrass. The first big-name act, the patriarchal "Mr. Bill" Monroe himself, wasn't to appear until Sunday.

Still, it cost 10 bucks per person to drive in and take a seat on one of the bowed planks set on concrete blocks in front of the glorified roadside stand of a stage. It would be as much as $15 on the heavy days, and $100 to stay for the duration.

Other evidence of big business was plentiful. It's hard to put a price on the privilege of sitting in a grove of towering trees, sipping a discreet beer under the NO ALCOHOL signs, and tasting the sweet syrup of fiddles and banjos played like they were born and not made. But the price at the "Largest Bluegrass Festival in USA" includes taco stands, Motley Crue T-shirts on sale and hired help wearing long-barreled revolvers.

Oh well, when you have thousands, you have hassles and maybe you need cops. Maybe you even have a market for Motley Crue T-shirts. Maybe that makes the opening day the best day, when a hard-core handful can settle back with coolers and lawn chairs and holler out requests without fear of being taken for a nuisance.

"Hey, you know what? The sun's coming out," Talmadge Law told his faithful audience midway through Friday's first show. "Bluegrass dries that rain right up, don't it?"

The dozens applauded, in no mood to doubt.

Listening for a Living

Plainfield, Ind. —Main Street is a shimmering desert on this last-gasp-of-August afternoon, but the Town Tavern is the same dim, cool sanctuary it has been for roughly a century.

Men and women of various ages, most of them in jeans, occupy a half-dozen of the stationary steel bar stools, their bottles of Budweiser and Pabst Blue Ribbon bejeweled by the fierce shaft of window light.

On the juke box, Willie Nelson and Merle Haggard are crooning about federales. In a booth near the back, George Washington Maupin is reminiscing about cops.

"Sap Franklin—of course, he was the chief back then—he'd have a few beers with the guys and then drive 'em home if they got drunk," Maupin says, contemplating the cigar that seems to grow out of his right hand.

"These cops nowadays, I don't know. It's like they have to act like they're better than you."

Well, says Bill Culver, the young proprietor, they're trained that way. Things are more formal now.

Maupin nods. He's seen 71 years' worth of change, 50 years of it from behind the bar of the Town Tavern. If anybody knows how to get along, it's somebody in his line of work.

"I've had troubles too, and I know it helps to talk about your troubles," he says of his countless customers. "One thing you learn is, you've got to listen to their troubles, but they don't want to hear yours."

George Maupin started listening on August 5, 1934, when

the first of a succession of "10 or 11" owners of the Town Tavern hired him on. He'd left his boyhood home in Kentucky hoping to find a job with an uncle in St. Louis; but when the freight train dumped him early, central Indiana became his future.

The nation was a year out of Prohibition then. A bottle of Oertel's 92 or Pabst or Champagne Velvet cost a dime, and George Maupin was paid a dollar for a 12-hour day — 10 to 10. Often, on his way home, he would make discreet deliveries to churchgoing folks who wouldn't dream of slaking their thirst for spirits in public.

The world's different now, but except for the video game in the back, where the steam table used to be, the Town Tavern looks much the same. And it ought to be said the barkeep, with his smooth face under thinning gray hair, his rolled shirtsleeves and breast pocket crammed with pens and cigars, carries his five decades pretty lightly as well.

"It went so fast I didn't realize it 'til the last few years," he reflects. "We never went hungry, but I had to work two jobs to do it. You don't have any choice when you raise nine kids."

Maupin says he could have bought the tavern 40 years ago and perhaps eliminated the need to supplement his income with odd jobs over the years. But his in-laws objected to that on religious grounds, and he respected their views.

He was married 36 years to his first wife, Lillian, who died nine years ago. Never, he says, did she taste alcohol. He himself enjoys a drink as much as anyone, he says, but he has never imbibed behind the bar.

Beyond that, George Maupin doesn't have a lot of rules. What it all boils down to, he says, is: "Treat everybody the way you would want to be treated."

Maupin now splits his weeks between Plainfield and his second home in Evansville. His present wife, Carol Sue, has been after him to retire and move to Florida. He will, he says, as soon as the Town Tavern changes owners again, which will be soon.

Bill Culver and his wife, Patty, have the establishment up for sale.

Maupin has been fighting the idea of retirement for several years. He calls the Culvers the nicest owners he's ever had. But not much else binds him to Plainfield. His kids are scattered, the juke box plays stuff he can't make heads or tales of, and the Sap Franklins, who "weren't afraid to let you be friendly," are long, long gone.

Weight of Tradition

The packed earth trembles a little from Green Lea Ike's friendly advance toward a visitor. The visitor trembles a little, too.

Green Lea Ike is just a two-year-old kid, full of joy and vinegar. He likes to dance around, check out shirt pockets, make some body contact. It matters nothing to him that he weighs more than half a ton and pounds around on iron-shod feet the size of a street lamp base.

The visitor gingerly pats the deep, flat neck and the quivering wall of shoulder. Ike, his sleek black hide glinting red from sunburn, snorts and veers away, more interested in the white-haired, bespectacled man who's raising him.

"He won two firsts over in Ohio," Ralph Coddington says, tapping his finger against Ike's rock-hard face, stroking his forelock, looking upward into his onyx marble eyes. "We're pretty proud of him—aren't we?"

Then he gives a sharp slap to the rubbery mouth, signaling that playtime is over. "Get away, now; go on." Ike turns grudgingly, then thumps along behind as Coddington moves to another stall to introduce another of his 15 purebred Percheron draft horses.

Blackhome Ryan, dapple gray, perhaps a full ton in weight, rattles the boards in his stall as he sidesteps the puny humans. "He's a good-dispositioned horse," Coddington says with a chuckle, "but when I got him bred to a mare, I've got a lot of different bits I've got to use to control him. I can't match him weight-wise."

Coddington, a spry and easy 69 years old, barely surpasses the newborns weight-wise. He has ushered a lot of them into the world, sometimes tying a rope to their hooves and pulling when the mother pushed, more often just being present while 2,000 pounds of nature took care of its own species preservation business.

The proprietor of Green Lea Farms was wielding the reins of draft horses before he started grammar school. He and his wife, Esther, have raised Percherons since their marriage in 1943 and have owned Green Lea Farms since 1949. Along with the three children who grew up there, Doretta, Laona, and James, they've won so many ribbons, trophies, and plaques at state fairs and other shows around the country they don't have room to display them all in their neat white house next to the barns and pasture.

Chances are you've seen Green Lea Farms. It's the place along I-65 near the Keystone exit where the older fellow (that would be Ralph Coddington) plows a corn stand and cuts hay behind draft horses. "I have people stop, look, get out, take pictures," he says. "There was little around us but woods when we came."

Horse-powered farming is uncommon enough in the country nowadays. In the city, it's practically a tourist attraction. Coddington didn't plan it that way—"The city kind of came to us."

He doesn't mind so much being surrounded by a residential neighborhood. He does mind what I-65 did. When the highway came through in the 1960s, it split Green Lea Farms, reducing its acreage from 55 acres to 45 and forcing Coddington to drive a mile and a half around to get to some of his herd—horses he can see and hear from his kitchen window.

Not that he's a holdout against progress. Coddington makes his living in the modern world, having been a manufacturer's sales representative the past 17 years after 27 years as a chemist. Percherons take up the evenings and the days off. Coddington breeds them, raises them, breaks them, shoes them, shows them, buys them, sells them, judges them, writes about them, consults about them. He is on the executive board of the Percheron Horse Association of America.

Coddington has judged horses in many states and in the United Kingdom. He has raised and driven teams that pulled the Indiana University calliope and wild-animal wagons in the Milwaukee, Wisconsin, circus parade. He's sold horses to the Indianapolis Zoo for its sightseeing coach and to the carriage ride companies. The other day, a man from Bogota, Colombia, stopped by for horse-buying advice, having heard of Coddington through the grapevine.

In numbers, Percherons rank second to Belgians among the massive work horses imported from Europe to modernize American farming in the mid-1800s. Today, draft horses are a specialty tool in agriculture; they are used, for example, on hilly ground, in some logging, and by Amish and ecology-minded traditional farmers.

Coddington remembers when tractors were new. His father worked his 260-acre farm entirely with Percherons, and that's how Coddington came to choose them as a hobby. He still has the red sleigh on which Percherons pulled him on dates a half-century of winters ago. The toy-sized conveyance cost him 50 cents.

Coddington sells between two and five horses a year at a price of $3,000 to $6,000, depending on whether a horse is sought for breeding, competitive pulling, show, or just work. His is a business of pleasure more than profit.

"I enjoy raising, breaking, and showing the horses," he says. "There is satisfaction in placing in a big show something you've bred and trained."

There are quieter satisfactions as well, felt when Coddington exercises his horses behind a hay mower or a corn binder that his father used, a piece of equipment older than he is.

"I wouldn't want to farm entirely with horses," he says, looking out over the hissing interstate that separates six of his Percherons, four in the east pasture and two on the hill to the west. "We've come too far for that. But I enjoy working with them. There's something more personable about it than sitting on a tractor."

The sweet, potent bouquet of hay and manure wafts from the stalls where more of his mighty horses await the nearing evening, when he will drive them to the field and present the commuters a living tableau on borrowed time.

"A lady called the other day and said, 'I heard you sold your place.' I told her, 'No, I'm still here.' She said, 'Oh, I'm so glad. I love to look at the horses.' But this will all be something else some day when I'm no longer around."

Royal Romance

Auburn, Ind. — By the hundreds, scattered over the sprawling, sunny grounds of Dekalb High School, the objects of America's love affair with the automobile await the answer to love's follow-up question:

OK, how much?

From the courtly esteem for a turn-of-the-century Rolls-Royce to the nostalgic puppy lust for a slightly rusty 1968 Pontiac Bonneville, affection for cars is being put on the scales for the world to see.

It's billed as the world's richest auction of collectors' cars. It's being run by Auburn's own Kruse International, world's biggest collector's car auctioneer.

It's Model Ts and T-Birds and Bugattis and even buses. It's the Rolls once driven by Jim and Tammy Bakker and the Cadillac limo that once carried Bobby Kennedy. It's six-figure Duesenbergs and glorified used cars.

It's hundreds of impassive faces, many belonging to people rich enough to buy Auburn and truck it away.

It's Dean V. Kruse himself, the thickset sales manager in the black tuxedo, working the mike as his tuxedo-clad minions patrol the crowd in the gym.

It's Friday, the beginning of another colossal Labor Day weekend sale, and Kruse is showing the form that once sold a Bugatti for $6.5 million.

"Sixty-seven, 67 now eight. Sixty-eight thousand, 68. Sixty-eight thousand, 68. Seventy thousand, now 71. I got 71, one of the finest *in the country. I got 71, two, three! I got 72, now 73. Roll it out. I got 72 now three. I got 72, 73, now four! I got 73, one of the finest in the country! A $100,000 car. I got 73, four, five. I got 75, 75, 75 . . . anybody else? Sold! To Marvin Friedman, the millionaire from Miami!"*

So there. In five minutes or so, a lovely white 1957 Mercedes-Benz 300L Roadster is betrothed to a wavy-haired Vince Edwards–lookalike from Florida.

Someday, maybe before the weekend is out, Marvin Friedman will resell the little jewel through his classic car dealership, perhaps using his own finance company. But it's not as though there's no feeling, he insists.

"It's a business, and a hobby too," says the millionaire in the red racing jacket. "As far as bidding advice goes, you have to have a figure in your mind. Our figure was 75. If the guy had gone $500 higher, he'd have had the car; but he doesn't know that."

Friedman has six cars of his own to run up Kruse's temporary revolving stage, including an Aston Martin with 22 taillights that was built for the late racer Graham Hill. He wants 100 grand for it.

Then there's "the fastest street-legal car in the world," a 1,200-horsepower Camaro Friedman claims to have driven in six $25,000 match races without a defeat.

"Once you grow up, life isn't as much fun any more," he confesses. "I'm still a little kid."

He's also a businessman whose antennae stay aquiver to the possibility of a certain car's appreciating $100,000 in a single week.

"The Japanese paid $42 million for a painting the other week at Christie's," Friedman says by way of illustration. "I love art, but you can't get in it and drive your friends around."

Speaking of which, Friedman says he promised his wife he'd get rid of the killer Camaro—for $150,000, negotiable.

Is it possible? "The whole world's car-crazy," Friedman says. This weekend, once again, he'll find out how much.

Laboring for the Lost

It's a summer night that weighs a ton. Ninety degrees and there ain't no breeze. Under a tent two stories tall, strung with naked light bulbs, the air entertains no movement, save for a few apathetic horseflies and that familiar old Southside sewer smell wafting over the faithful.

Brother Roger Mullins from Madisonville, Kentucky, is on stage at Indianapolis Baptist Temple—coat off, vest unbuttoned, necktie at half-staff, silver-rimmed glasses gone from his square, glistening face. Only his swept-back brown hair remains dry and undisturbed. Behind him is a banner stretching the width of the tent, sounding a warning from Romans 3:23: *"For all have sinned and come short of the glory of God."*

The evangelist glares out over several hundred men, women, and children in wooden folding chairs—alert, scrubbed people, some in jeans and T-shirts but most of them dressed for church and the heat in whites and pastel pinks and greens. They use funeral parlor fans, song lists, and Bibles to stir the thick air as the preacher rains down on lukewarm Christians.

"The devil has some of us in a trance, believe it or not. In a spiritual, in a devil-like amnesia. . . . I mean, boy, you think, 'Well, I been good, I been doing good deeds for other people,' and you think when it comes time for you to die, a lot of people think, 'God's gonna just turn his head and let me in the back door.' You got another think comin', friend. . . . HEY, LISTEN, I've got NEWS for ya, you'll either come through the blood of Christ or you'll BURN IN HELL!"

"Yeah!" someone shouts. "Amen!" Brother Mullins' clear,

nasal Dixie voice climbs from a whisper to a shriek and drops back again—over and over—as he paces alone across the pulpit punching the air.

"You think, 'Well, everything's going my way, I don't have any problems, any trials.' Hey! You better look out! There's a shock treatment HEADIN' YOUR WAY!"

For nearly two hours he works, mixing fire from the pulpit and sweet gospel music performed with his wife and young son and daughter. The Roger Mullins Family—they have a whole stack of albums and tapes for sale after the service. But record purchases are not the fruit by which the evangelist's labors are judged. The reckoning comes in the final minutes of his sermon, when those who are moved to proclaim their acceptance of his message will walk the sawdust center aisle.

Brother Roger Mullins is near tears as they make their way up, one and two at a time, slowly separating themselves from the security of the sea of seats.

"How can you sit there? Christ spoke to your heart, and yet you rebel. You might just think I'm sittin' up here hollerin' and sayin' words. I can show you many, many times, and many, many people, where God's given the shock treatment."

Against a processional of anvil-like piano notes, they come forward—a young man in a fringed leather vest; an old man in a blue and yellow tropical shirt, lurching behind a cane; a teenage girl in a black T-shirt that says "KC and the Sunshine Band" on the front.

"IT'S SAD TO KNOW THAT CHRIST HAS SPOKEN TO YOU TO-NIGHT, AND YET —you keep rebelling . . ."

Another comes, and another, perhaps a half-dozen in all, most of them young. Sheree, Buddy, and Cindy Mullins are singing "Lord, I'm Coming Home" as they march. Roger Mullins is weeping.

"Before somebody gets home tonight, Lord, the shock treatment's gonna hit him . . . suddenly, Lord, something's gonna happen to

us that we don't realize. O God, give us some people that's not ashamed. . . ."

He's winding down now. His slender harvest is complete, and the comparative coolness of the outside beckons. Already, headlights are flaring under a starry pewter sky. Smiling, chatting Christians make their way across the grass and gravel. It has been a blazing July night, and tomorrow is a work day . . .

Corners

City Fishing

An ill wind is blowing bad luck across the mud-green surface of the Indianapolis Water Co. canal, where Bobby Mills is trying for channel catfish with mashed minnows on the hook.

People say you can get catfish long as your arm out of this water, and crappies and bluegills and big ugly carp, when the weather's warm and the wind isn't kicking up. But this is one of those days, Mills says, when "it's almost like the fish are watching you, man."

Mills and his girlfriend, Leslie Dodd, who is casting for crappies a few yards to the north, pass the minutes in silence. The chilly gusts rolling over the 16th Street bridge break the dense water like gravel and bounce a half-submerged wine bottle against the bank, as if offering it up as a substitute for fish. Beer cans and paper bait cups memorialize the countless other fishermen who've taken this gravel back road in the heart of the city.

His rod and reel propped against a chunk of concrete, Mills squints from beneath his light blue fishing hat across the grayish water, toward the dam and Pennyman's Body Shop, and tells how he started fishing off the canal with his grandfather when he was 9 years old.

Now 24, he remembers when you could "tear the hell out of some bluegills," back before they built the interstate and dumped all that dirt and gravel in the canal.

Whatever they say about pollution and such, the canal is still good fishing, he says. He likes it better than Eagle Creek, because there's no limit; better than pay lakes, because there's more of a challenge.

Suddenly, he turns and bolts toward his pole, anchored a few feet away from him on the ground.

Throwing himself down behind it, spread-eagled like a machine-gunner, he watches the line stretch and twitch and then fall limp again. He keeps watching. He spits a couple times for luck. "He didn't get all of it! He'll come back. Betcha he'll come back."

"He" does come back, eventually, but he's not a 3-pound catfish. He's a baby bluegill, golden against the gray sky, hardly larger than the minnow he swallowed. Mills laughs and tries to remove the hook to give the fish a shot at maturity, but he can't save it. So, the bluegill will become the bait.

Mills lays the flopping critter on a slab of concrete and then stamps it once, twice, three times with his left sneaker, turning it into a stringy red mass of garbage. "Cats like that slimy stuff," he says, casting it back into the water.

The best time to get catfish, according to Mills, is about 4 in the morning. The best place is over by the filtration plant, where the fish feed on refuse that gets trapped by the screens.

A lot of folks would say no time's a good time to fish in these murky inner city waters. Or at least, nothing swimming in there they'd care to eat. That's fine with Mills.

"I have people say that to me all the time. They say the fish that comes out of the canal and out of White River tastes oily. It's not that the fish tastes oily. It's just an old saying that's been around so long it's programmed into people's minds. Not the older people, though."

The older people remember when the canal was clear water, Mills says. But even now, after its best days, he'll bet you that you can go to some spots and pull out a half-dozen big healthy bass.

"I go fishing with my grandfather up to Toledo, in Lake Michigan, and by the time you get that boat down to the water, it's the same as this. Water is water. Fish is fish."

And wind isn't worth fighting. The evening crowd of fellow anglers—old men, mothers, children—is starting to trickle in when Bobby and Leslie decide to call it quits for awhile.

They'll return after dark, when the wind's died down, when the mean old denizens of industrial waters are more hungry than smart.

Sub-minimum Wage

Standing on a near-Downtown sidewalk in the golden warmth of a perfect fall day, Jack and Jo Ann roll up their left sleeves to compare needle marks.

"You can hardly fine a vein anymore," Jack says, tracing the tributaries of scar tissue that run along his tanned forearm.

Smirking at the challenge, Jo Ann holds up her skinny arm. It is starkly gray in the glittering sunshine, and in its crook is a squarish hole that could have been made by a small chisel—or by seven years of needles.

Years of needles, years of need.

Jack, Jo Ann, and Jo Ann's husband, Fred, are in line at the Hyland Laboratories Plasma Center on East Washington Street to deliver their twice weekly pints of blood. The whole process including the waiting will take about five hours and pay them $10 apiece, which makes this one of the lowest paid part-time jobs on the market.

For someone who just needs a bottle and a pack of cigarettes it's not a bad wage. But for these three people, the needle cannot begin to fill the hole.

"I made $23,000 in 1978 and $20,000 in 1979," Fred says blankly. "I never dreamed I'd be making nothing in 1982."

He gazes into the passing traffic through thick, black-framed glasses. "All these people driving by, laughing and pointing—they ought to know it isn't just winos who come here."

Fred says he has been coming to Hyland for about a year. Before that, he was a machine operator at a large automotive parts

plant—a skilled worker, a member of the Steelworkers Union
with 12 years' seniority.

The layoff came a year and a half ago. Since then, he's tried
the temporary help people, the state spot labor agency, and the
township trustee. He's come away with next to nothing. Since
his unemployment benefits ran out, he and Jo Ann have been
living with his sister.

"The trustee says you have to make 10 [job] applications a
week to be eligible for help." his wife says. "What are you going
to do when you run all over town and when you get there they
won't even let you fill out an application?"

Fred remembers going to the spot labor office at 4 a.m., two
hours before it opened. "Some days they wouldn't send anybody
out at all. So I started coming to the plasma joint."

In these times, the plasma joint draws a mixed group of sup-
pliers. As Fred and Jo Ann sit on a stoop outside and she bends
over a pink paperback novel called *Ashes in the Wind,* Jack paces
in white loafers, pulling on his pipe and smiling wryly.

Nearby, a middle-aged man in a blue T-shirt stands with arms
folded over his pot belly, a newspaper poking from one front
pocket and Erica Jong's *Fear of Flying* from the other.

Two tall, thin young men with trimmed hair and clean, casual clothes wait near the doorway to the small crowded storefront, as if embarrassed to be in the sunlight.

When an old man in round glasses passes by, clutching his
blood money, Jack chortles: "Don't go get drunk now." The gent
laughs dryly and replies: "This is going for food."

After 15 years, off and on, Jack is pretty much a fixture at the
plasma joint. It's not as though he hasn't had good jobs. He carries a card that identifies him as "a certified engineer in the state
of Tennessee." But the jobs are always temporary, and he has this
"damn drinking" to contend with.

Fred, who at 43 is seven years younger than Jack, has no desire to become a fixture.

His escape route is a class in computer programming that

starts in November at Indiana Vocational Technical College, but he's waiting on his application for a grant.

"I'm one of those people that's looked quite a bit. I'm what they call a discouraged job seeker now. Your clothes get baggy, your shoes get run down. You just generally look like hell."

With Election Day approaching, he is asked what he thinks of all those politicians who claim to be riding to the rescue of the unemployed.

He turns away, his jaw rigid. "I've got no comment on that."

Jo Ann, meanwhile, has gone inside to check the progress of the line. She returns, holding her novel open, squinting into the sunlight.

"Fifteen more minutes," she tells Fred.

Bearing the News

Jackhammers gnaw the half-devoured carcass of the Board of Trade Building, raising such a rude racket that Clarence Weber must shout to make conversation from his ringside seat across Ohio Street.

He gives no sign that the demolition noise bothers him, just as he pays no attention to the deafening soul music that pours forth from a teenager's stereo box to invade his green and white hut.

A warm, sunny day with commotion on the sidewalks is bread and butter for the round, smiling man in the plaid shirt and tweed cap. He spends 12 hours a day thrusting newspapers, magazines, and puzzle books into the flow of humanity around Ohio and Meridian Streets, and he only wishes the flow were heavier.

"I'm not making no money," he yells. "The newspaper business is shot. When I first came, I'd sell 75–85 of *The News* a day. I'd sell a hundred *Stars*. But it's fell way down. People are out of work. Where they'd buy two papers a day before, maybe they'll be lucky to buy one. Maybe they won't come downtown at all."

Bearing down on his 80th birthday, Weber isn't sure how much longer he'll stay in the free-standing newsstand business, which has few practitioners left downtown. "I should quit," he says. "It's a dog's life."

He pauses to greet a chipper young woman who wants copies of *People* magazine and *The Indianapolis News*.

"Getting some sunshine?" he croons to her.

"It's so pretty, I hate to go back inside," she cries.

"Well then, why don't you play hooky?"

"I wish I could," she says, her laughter trailing behind her as she rejoins the sparse early afternoon traffic.

Weber's trade was much better during the five years the stand was across the street and the Board of Trade Building was occupied. The office workers alone were good for 25 papers a day, and the drugstore at street level drew a sizable crowd.

Eight weeks ago, the demolition project forced Weber to move his little shack, with its window displays of the *Saturday Evening Post, Muscle Digest* and the *Sporting News.* Having the lawn of the Federal Courts Building behind him, instead of a tall building and a row of stores, he now gets more wind, more rain, and less business.

Weber has a better location in mind, elsewhere in the downtown area. If the city licensing authorities are agreeable, he says, he'll give it another shot. If they seem to prefer coin boxes to a human vendor, he'll just quit the business.

"It's a dog's life. If you want to make a few nickels at it, you've gotta stay here all the time. If you don't, they'll steal a third of your papers."

With difficulty, he twists around on his stool in the 6-foot-by-9-foot shed and points toward the side window, curtained by tabloids and magazines.

"I've had to put in three of those windows. They cost $75–80 a throw by the time you pay for the labor and all." He waves toward the box office window in the front above a counter littered with coins.

"They'll break in here and steal a bunch of these books. If they get 30 books at $2.50 to $3 a book, there goes everything I made."

Weber has made better money than this. He's been a steel warehouse worker, a construction worker, and an apartment house manager. He quit the last job because he got tired of the vandalism by some of the tenants. Then he got tired of staying home alone.

Being out has its price. In the wintertime, it's dark when Weber hangs his can on the back wall alongside the discreet display of girlie magazines, and dark again when he takes it down to go home. The $1.50 a day for fuel for the Coleman heater puts a severe dent in his profits.

Then comes spring, when transistorized music punches the air, customers pause to chat, and thoughts of retiring return to the shelf.

"It's a dog's life, I kind of like it," the old man says with a smile. "It keeps you up with the public. I can't get work anywhere else at my age, and I don't like to sit around. I like to drink beer, but you can't depend on that. You got to take care of yourself."

On the Urban Frontier

They put James and Peggy Casey on the TV news when they bought their house on East 32nd Street back in 1975. They were urban pioneers, ripping the boards off the windows and setting out to resurrect a ratty corpse of a building.

Fourteen years later, they have a proud monument to their sweat and cost. The massive two-story frame dwelling, repainted just last year in deep blue with white trim, seems like a mirage in a neighborhood of broken windows and vacant lots and scruffy cars full of idle young men.

Inside, the laborious facelift is most obvious in the deep brown paneling that coats the two main downstairs rooms. The effect might be pretty somber if it were not offset by colorful memorabilia from the Caseys' three athletic sons—a University of Kentucky wall clock, a football team photo from Park Tudor School, trophies and ribbons.

All is in place for this gentle retired couple, watching television in late afternoon as a son and grandson chase around upstairs.

All, including the deer rifle propped against the front room chair and the ashtray filled with bullets.

"I like to keep it where I can reach it, because you never know when you might need it," James Casey says. "These dope people will do some funny things."

Through his picture window he can see the dilapidated house across the street where a small army of police arrested two people the other day on charges of cocaine possession.

Police said they believed the suspects wanted to use the building as a "crack house" for selling drugs. The concrete block fortress the occupants built around the front door, for a house that doesn't even have glass in a lot of its windows, was taken as a pretty good clue.

The Caseys say they haven't seen any narcotics, but they've suspected the hovel across the street for three months or so. "People going in there day and night, cars pulling up, it lets you know something's going on that's unusual," James Casey says.

"This was not a Church of God neighborhood when we moved in, but it was not like it is now."

Six feet, 6 inches tall, with a deep steady voice and a ready laugh, Casey does not wear his fear on his sleeve. But the fear is real.

"We do go to church a lot," he says, "and when you get home you never know who you're going to face. . . . I don't fear for myself as much as for my family. If I get mobbed or gunned down for what's right, well, somebody's got to take a stand."

The Caseys say they haven't been directly affected by the drug traffic they suspect or by the gunshots they hear at night. A few items stolen from the yard, a car broken into. But they believe they have at least two dope houses, not just the one across the street but a place behind them as well. "If they shoot at each other and hit you," Casey says, "you're just as dead."

They have sacrificed to spare their sons. While their eldest stayed with his grandmother and went to school in Kentucky, the second son graduated from Park Tudor and their youngest is a freshman at the exclusive, expensive private school a healthy distance north of 32nd Street.

"When my son's friends come home with him, I have to make sure they all get in the house safely," Peggy Casey says. "It's embarrassing."

Her husband says he's tried to get his decent neighbors to act on the deterioration that closes in on his beloved house, but nobody wants to get involved. He's sure he'll never get his investment out of the place, but the Marine Corps veteran of the Korean War says he isn't leaving unless he gets "burnt out or shot out."

He drops wearily onto the arm of a couch and gazes out at the fortified dump where the arrests took place hours before. "Hopefully," he sighs, "I'll be able to get a good night's sleep tonight."

Outside, a few minutes later, a young man from the neighborhood pauses in his walk past the house with the concrete reinforced door.

"You a reporter?" he asks, spotting the notebook and flashing a smile that seems not so much cocky as fatalistic. "This guy say he'll be back in business by 12 noon tomorrow."

Pets at Rest

The six mausoleums on the grounds of Memory Gardens are less than a mile from the go-go bars and gas stations of Pendleton Pike, but they luxuriate in peace.

Melvin Barnes, the caretaker, trudges through the untouched foot-deep snow toward the family crypt of the Frankforts, who established the cemetery 20 years ago. He directs a visitor to the pink marble slabs bearing the names of the four loved ones entombed there, Sugar Frankfort, Dixie Frankfort, Wah Wah and Scampy Frankfort.

"We got one lady—Davis, I think her name is. Lives in California. She's got about five reserved here. Whenever one dies, she brings 'im here all the way from California."

Barnes has one here himself. "Just a little hound dog," he says. "Had him 17 1/2 years. No tellin' how long he'd have lived if he hadn't got a tumor. He's buried right over there."

Buried with about 5,000 other pets—dogs and cats, mostly, but parakeets too, and rabbits and monkeys. Buried along with Stitches Taylor, whose stone marker bears a plastic wreath and the message: "We love and miss you, Puppy."

Buried near the stately tombs of Pouchie McAnany (1962–1969), and Humperdinck Abell (1969–1978), and Countess Melissa Heather Klotz (1963–1972).

Laid to rest with reverence and expense that bespeak genuine grief.

It costs from $100 to $150, depending on the size of the animal, to bury a pet in Memory Gardens. Entombment is $350. It is safe to say most animal lovers have less love than that.

Yet considering that burial is done in a cement vault and the mausoleum fee includes a metal container and inscribed marble seal, it seems certain no one is getting rich off the bereaved.

As a matter of fact, Memory Gardens is a nonprofit concern—a 10-acre monument to the memory of Leona Frankfort, whose death occurred three years ago last Wednesday and whose life was a working definition of "humane." Mrs. Frankfort spend 22 years in the Indianapolis Police Department, first as a juvenile probation officer and then as a dog pound superintendent. After her retirement in 1947, she put her concern for the vulnerable into practice by buying the farm on Pendleton Pike and establishing a kennel for homeless animals there. The cemetery was a logical outgrowth.

Neither the living nor the dead has gotten short shrift. The cemetery always has had a resident caretaker in the large white farmhouse with miniature caskets on its front porch. The strays—there are 10 in residence now—always have been treated to air-conditioning and home cooking.

"They can't be makin' any money," Melvin Barnes says, ushering an obese, yelping mixed breed into the back door of the house. "She just couldn't stand to see a stray dog running loose."

The torch is carried now by Barnes and Marty Frankfort, the widower of the founder. Marty is 85 and rarely gets to the cemetery from his Northside home. Barnes brings the receipts over every week, then takes the proceeds to the bank after Marty pays the bills.

The payroll covers Barnes and another man who dig the graves by hand (the largest are 52 inches long, 28 inches wide, and 3 feet deep). Other expenses include such unbudgeted necessities as repair of the short north wall of sandstone and ornamental iron, which has suffered countless encounters with traffic from the motel next door.

The wall looks perfect now. When it crumbles again, it will be repaired again. As long as there is a Frankfort in charge, the line will be preserved between the gray slush of the street and the silent estate where plastic bouquets poke through the smooth snow like overeager crocuses.

How could Leona Frankfort rest in peace if Little Joe Peters, Princess Ann Cole, and Happy Wolff My Sunshine were denied that right?

Soul Man

Our guided tour of Faith Teaching Church of Deliverance starts out back, where dead bottles of Colt .45 and Olde English 800 malt liquor put faith to the eye test.

The Reverend Shedrick Madison, wide as his vision, a squiggly-haired man with a bear's body under his pink dress shirt and necktie, looks past the piles of trash to see the future. One day, Lord willing, this will be a tot park.

"We want to make the corner live," the pastor says. "We want to resurrect it."

Inside the dim, musty storefront church, where six rows of folding chairs flanked by kerosene space heaters face a borrowed pulpit, the vision shifts to the open front door.

Young guys are hanging out, and long cars are pausing in the weekday afternoon sunshine on the corner of 40th Street and Boulevard Place. One of the young guys is talking into a portable phone, probably not to his mom. A few yards away, a beauty shop is open for business—but locked for caution.

"I want to give kids an alternative to what they're already seeing," Madison says. "Once the crack man gets them in, you'll never get them out. The bucks are too big. Kids are making $15,000 to $20,000 a day selling drugs."

The pastor prays every day for less money than that. Among other modest desires, he wants to fix up his church with some real pews, obtain maybe 100 Bibles, find a second van to supplement his Dodge Ram with its 140,000 miles, start a high school equivalency degree program, and scare up some good used audio and video gear to compete with the crack man for bodies and souls.

"I want to take it to the street, the message that Jesus Christ is Lord, that there's another way besides death and destruction. I want to get a sound truck, park it in, say, Tarkington Park. It would be the sounds they want to hear, but to glorify God. I could bring Christian rappers in.

"This is the video age. People think I'm crazy wanting to use computers and all this stuff. But you've got to reach young people in a different way. If 2 Live Crew can have range expanders, the church should have range expanders."

Outside in his prayer-powered brown beater of a van, Madison shows evidence of another way he gets the message across — pictures and posters from his second career, as "Big Red the Wrestling Preacher."

A product of the 33rd Street and Washington Boulevard area, "back when a neighborhood was a family," Madison wrestled at North Central High School and has done it professionally since 1980, mostly around the Midwest. He owes his nickname to his red costumes and to the ministerial work that began in 1982 and saw him ordained in 1985.

Nowadays, at 33, with bad knees, he climbs into the ring sporadically, and he does it as an evangelistic tool. He has a wrestling show scheduled for June 13 in nearby Andrew Ramsey Park. It is one of several outreach efforts he's made with community groups and larger churches.

"I'm trying to maintain a basketball program," he adds as he steers the van from the corner and down a quiet side street, "with guys 19 and 20 years old. It lets me talk to them. Sometimes I get out there with them, but my knees . . ."

His laughter stops as the park looms in the windshield.

"See what happened? They took the goals down. I can see their reasoning. People were hanging out selling drugs. But now the kids have no place to play ball."

No place to play, because kicking kids out of parks is cheaper for the city than supervising them. No place to work, because skills and education don't keep up with energy. No escape from the threat of drugs, because "they don't stop it at the source, and the source isn't here."

The van winds past Ramsey Park to the home of a parishioner named Bill Lowe, who meets the minister on the front porch and watches the afternoon action with him. Guys and thumping cars on another corner.

"There's Cowboy," Bill says, his speech slowed by the effects of a gunshot wound to the head three years ago. "I ain't seen him since Jug died."

Jug was David A. Moore, 31. He was shot to death a few months back, near the door of Faith Teaching Church of Deliverance. Nobody has been arrested. Police say drugs were involved, but they don't say he had a lot of cash on him. The word on the street is he had $27,000.

"It's a war," Big Red the Preacher declares, pumping his hamhock fists. "Like the Bible says, it's good vs. evil, love vs. hate."

Right now, good is broke. Much as Madison would like to claim a congregation of 500, with a Sunday collection that would cover a computer or a good used van, he is proud of the 50 to 70 souls he's enfolded since opening his church in July.

"You can't put a price on a Bill Lowe"—who, like the pastor, lives in the neighborhood and shows his face to the crack man.

Pushing the Dodge Ram south along Central Avenue, on his way to negotiate for some used pews a wealthy church is discarding, the wrestling preacher spots a familiar scene: A liquor store parking lot, busy with idle men.

"That's what I want," he says. "I want to get in that lot right across from 500 Liquor. I'd get a permit and play what they want to hear. I'd draw them to me. Maybe I'd get one out of 15 of 'em, or one out of 100. What price do you put on that? I know I'd get one. I'd get two, because I'm greedy."

Man of War

He takes one more swig from his 40-ouncer, still wrapped in a brown paper bag, and dumps the last couple inches onto the cracked pavement for the sun and dust to claim.

All of us watching know beer's not the worst stain that's been on this parking lot.

"Got to pour some out," the man with the 40-ouncer says, "for my dead homes."

Pouring out beer for lost homes—home boys, friends—is a gang ritual of long standing; but probably not in this case. These shootings and stabbings weren't gang-related, for the most part. Besides, libations for fallen comrades go back thousands of years. One more thing that's not new in the neighborhood, like violent death.

The 40-ounce man, 20 years old, has known more people dead before their time than the average veteran of the Persian Gulf War. This is no exaggeration. He thinks of the dead, and himself, as statistics.

"The black male is messed up," he says, though he uses a stronger word than "messed."

It's not the street expletive that strikes me. It's the other part. "The black male" sounds odd coming from a real person. It's the categorical jargon of sociologists and newspapers.

Well, he reads newspapers, and on those occasions when what he reads squares with his experience, he picks up the language and enriches it with his own.

"Pour some out for my dead homes"—corny, if the casualties

were not real. A bunch of us can stand there without fear in the afternoon sun, children can play kickball a few feet away, school buses can squeal to a stop on either side of us, but the persistence of routine living doesn't mean it's not a war zone. Children walk to school past burning cars in Beirut. Children kicked soccer balls in Baghdad between waves of bombers.

I remember something another fellow told me in another neighborhood. "There's a war coming," he said. "People have got to have it, and they'll get it any way they can."

Maybe it's coming, and maybe it's already on.

There's a conspiracy theory in the inner city about drugs and booze. You'll hear people say all those discount liquor stores with guys in the parking lots are there to pacify the population. And drugs? Everybody knows the big money ends up far away, and many suspect the government is in on the trade. Wasn't Manuel Noriega our boy when he was running drugs through Panama? Where did the cocaine finally get retailed?

It doesn't take drugs or drug money to get you killed here. It doesn't take much of anything. Middle-class society can feign aversion to violence because it's shielded from its consequences; but outside the walls, violence is an ordinary phenomenon for many people from a very early age.

One day, you see a home for the last time. Next day, you pour some out for him. It's a tradition about as old as war.

In the parking lot, in the sunshine, the guy waves his 40-ouncer and his pack of Kools at some junior high school kids. He is big, good with words, is liked and is listened to.

"You think I ought to be out here doing this?" he demands.

"It's what you choose to do," one of the kids replies.

"But you know it's wrong, right?"

The boys look at him in silence. They knew the same dead men he knew. They are too young and too old to tell him he is alive and wrong.

Haunted Houses

It happened to be Halloween when George and Gretchen Platzer got off the ship in New York City during the first decade of this century.

"Papa, let's go back!" Gretchen cried in German as costumed revelers swirled around them. "Everybody's crazy here!"

Having forsaken their tiny town in Bavaria for the huge promise of America, the young couple could go any direction but back. With their four-year-old son, Ernest, and Gretchen's elderly mother, Margaret Dengler, they were headed far inland, to a place less frightening than New York.

By the recollection of their only surviving child, that was about 1905. Indianapolis was barely a city beyond the Mile Square. The Platzers moved into an apartment above a drugstore on Alabama Street just south of 16th Street, where two more sons, Emil and George, were born.

Soon the family purchased a grand Italianate house at 1610 North Alabama. The senior Platzer made the front into his store and built onto the back for his bakery. A daughter, Elsa, was born in that house filled with oven smells.

The business flourished for many years, then went the way of most family-owned bakeries in the age of mass production. The neighborhood changed, the parents and grandmother died, the children grew up and moved away.

Except Emil.

"He was so sentimental about the homestead," says Elsa Yensel, 76, who now lives in Melbourne, Florida. "I'd begged him to move and come here and live with me. He just wouldn't hear of it."

Emil Platzer never married and never moved from the complex of three massive pre-1900 houses into which the homestead evolved—1610, 1614, and 1620 North Alabama. He went through hell to stay there.

A Metro bus once crashed into his living room.

A drunken driver ran over him when he was 70 years old, forcing him to go about on two canes for the last eight years of his life.

People broke into the houses and ripped him off and beat him up, nobody knows how many times.

They would take his tools while he was working under his car. They would steal things from his pickup truck while he was in the house unloading groceries.

When it came to problems, however, he wasn't just a recipient.

Platzer was a collector. His rooms and yard were piled high with possessions, precious to him but of mixed quality to an outsider. He had unopened boxes of power tools and stacks of good wood with which he planned to restore the century-old houses. He also had lots of cats and lots of trash.

Neighbors complained. The authorities issued cleanup orders. Emil Platzer ignored the orders, though he was seen on his roof, with his canes, making repairs.

Once, when the city cleaned up his yard over his protests, entire automobiles were found under the debris. Auto mechanics was among his many skills.

"He was very intelligent, spoke very well and was very much with it," an attorney for the Marion County Health and Hospital Corp. recalled after many battles. "He just simply liked to keep all his personal collections and possessions around him."

Health and Hospital obtained a court guardianship for Platzer at one point, but the Probate Court ended it when the old man demonstrated he was competent.

"He didn't smoke, drink or hurt anyone," his sister says. "He had a heart of gold and worked like a beaver. This is the result."

On March 19, 1986, police found Emil Platzer's burned body under a pile of trash in the house at 1614 North Alabama. Robbers had clubbed him to death and then set a fire.

Two men were charged with a litany of felonies. Because one of them changed the story he originally told on the other, and because there were no other witnesses, the prosecutor's office settled for guilty pleas to theft and burglary.

As far as Elsa Yensel is concerned, her prediction to a detective that the suspects would "come out smelling like a rose" was on the money. Her attorney shares her disgust.

So great was Emil Platzer's portion of injustice, Gustin J. Raikos says, it has outlived him.

"He was born in the area, raised in the area, loved the area," the attorney says. "He was beaten with a two-by-four and killed. They have a videotaped confession. They get a reduced sentence through a plea agreement and we're still struggling."

The struggle is over the houses. Mrs. Yensel, who lost her husband three months before her brother's murder, is unable to rehabilitate the structures and has been unable to find a buyer. The estate has spent thousands of dollars on trash-hauling alone, but the complaints about leaky roofs, weeds, and vagrants keep coming.

The Indianapolis Historic Preservation Commission approved a city request to demolish 1610, the house Elsa was born in. Such approval is required because of its age (circa 1875) and its location in a historic district. The outlook for the other two gray, paintless buildings is not bright, though restoration wonders have been worked in the area.

Elsa Yensel says she will listen to any offer. She treasures her memories of the German-English harmonies around the dinner table and the bubbling vat over which she helped her father make doughnuts. But the homestead itself is just a burden, a ghastly reminder that evil sometimes wins, that life in America could indeed be crazy.

The Scoop from Snookie

"I got 3 cents in my pocket and I'm standing there talking to a kid who pulls out a wad with $5,000. But when the cops vamp on you, it's gone. You'll be 40 years old and a slave because you got no education."

Charles "Snookie" Hendricks is at home on a sidewalk at 39th and Illinois streets, pacing and waving and "what's happenin'-ing" to about everybody who passes by and sharing his fat wad of views on the state of the neighborhood and world.

"Poor white America is headed for servitude; poor black America is headed for slavery," says the man in motion with the gray goatee and the blue leather Muslim cap pinned with a gold key to the city. "I won't live to see it, but it's coming."

Snookie Hendricks has lived and seen from top to bottom in this city. He was pretty much Mr. Black Militant during the yeasty late 1960s and early '70s, the man white politicians and do-gooders had to see if they wanted to reach angry black youths and a substantial portion of the black electorate. Snookie can drop names; shoot, he can drop nicknames, from Dick Lugar to Steve Goldsmith. Dick the senator; Steve the mayor; Dick and Steve and Snookie.

Snookie still can get VIPs on the phone once in a while. He's been meeting with some church leaders about his plan to turn a storefront into a recreation spot for the teenagers who worry him so much.

But Snookie isn't the man to see in the 1990s. He says he's on the street these days because he won't stand in a welfare line.

He says he's spreading the same message to kids, even if the big shots are gone.

"The game ain't changed. Different players, but the game ain't changed. They've just upped the tempo. In the late '60s, the weapon was a revolutionary-type thing. You wouldn't turn a gun on your own kind so much as on what was against you. Now, the dollar has become God and the gun is to protect it. There's no political awareness no more."

Can he bring that to kids? Is that what he wants? Opinions always have been mixed about Snookie Hendricks. He did time for drugs on various occasions. His connections Downtown got him suspected of being an informant. His organizing work with rebellious youths got him branded a troublemaker.

"If I'm an informant," he demands on the street corner, "where's my money?"

As for his approach to kids, well, take it or leave it.

"I asked this bunch of men the other day, 'What would you do if you saw a bunch of kids smoking reefer?' One of them says, 'Tell 'em to throw it away.' Another one says, 'I'd cuss 'em out.' One of them asks me what I'd do, and I say, 'I'd sit down and smoke it with 'em, but I'd tell them why it's wrong.'

"You can't talk to 'em if you run 'em off; you can't talk to 'em if you're cussin.'

"I want a place where the old men and the kids can gather. The old men could tutor them. What happened to teaching? There's no history if the old aren't teaching the young. They don't know who Bill Robinson is. They don't know who Lena Horne is."

Snookie Hendricks is 60. He says he's been on the street since he was 11. He says an Army hospital screw-up in 1948 hooked him on heroin, and conversion to Islam from the "hypocrisy" of Christianity helped him shake it. He says the ice cream cone he's licking is "one of the last things on the planet I still enjoy." He also says he has 24 children out there, including a 7-year-old girl who wants a computer.

"I got to get it," he says over the traffic, between salutes. "She's got a good mother. A damn good mother. Father's not so bad either."

A Chance to Go Your Way

On a gray October afternoon at Veterans Memorial Plaza, when the wind through the rows of flags sings an ominous prelude to winter, an angel of mercy meets the Angel of Death.

The angel of mercy is a green-eyed woman in jeans who pops out of the Mission on Wheels truck when it lumbers to its daily stop at the edge of the park, where a line of hungry people awaits. "Nurse Anne" is printed in red letters on a sticker on her dark blue sweater, near where a crucifix and a dove medallion hang.

The other angel actually is named Anthony, but they call him Angel, short for Angel of Death, because he says he went out at night and killed people in Vietnam. He wears a grimy Indianapolis Colts cap over a thin caramel face with gray stubble between goatee and sideburns. He is in bad shape.

Anne Farringer, R.N., helps Angel over to the grass and clicks her pen. Half-sitting, half-lying, he brings her up to date. He just spent two weeks in the hospital with flashbacks, and that's not all.

"I got shot in the leg two weeks ago, down on the Avenue."

"Who did it?"

"Don't know. Don't care."

She asks him where he is living. He points to the sidewalk.

"On the street?"

"Yes. Like to froze to death last night."

"Can you get in one of those missions?"

"Can't."

"Why?"

"My attitude. Getting in fights."

"What will you do this winter?"

"Die, I guess."

"You got through Nam," the nurse exclaims with a come-off-it kind of laugh. "You're a survivor, right?"

"Yeah," he says, finally smiling too.

A bright green sweater, donated by a church member somewhere, lies across his bony knees. She gives him two Tylenol tablets for his aching leg and he washes them down with red punch from the Mission on Wheels.

"It sure doesn't pay a lot," Anne Farringer says later. "But that doesn't make any difference. It's the personal reward, the sense of achievement, that a person in crisis or need can be made a little better, something I do can make a difference."

Farringer, 41, holder of a master's degree in counseling, veteran of the Peace Corps and the Wishard Memorial Hospital emergency room, is on the streets these days. She is part of a four-member team from People's Health Center that takes medical care and social service out to the homeless.

Funded under the federal Stewart B. McKinney Homeless Assistance Act, the Homeless Initiative Program pays weekly visits to seven shelters for the homeless, from the missions for men to a sanctuary for abused women and children. In addition, Farringer rides with Mission on Wheels, a Christian volunteer service, every Thursday. On her own, she also may start hitting a hole in the wall down on South Street where a bunch of old fellows hide from the wind.

"You learn about these places by grapevine and by default," she says. "If you're going to serve the populations, you need to be flexible."

The flexibility extends to the mind as well. Stereotypes about drunken bums fail to hold up, not only because a guy who is drunk and on the bum is also an individual, but because he shares the street nowadays with women and children.

"What surprised me is the education level of the people we've seen," says Judith K. Watt, R.N., who directs the homeless program for People's Health Center. "More than 50 percent have at least a high school education. Some have bachelor's degrees, master's degrees. There are lots of reasons for homelessness."

Money is a reason, one that many people who clip past Angel and Anne Farringer in store-bought shoes may not care to concede.

"I have come to the realization," Anne Farringer says, "that there are many problems that exist, some of which we can Band-aid, others of which are chronic and take a long time, i.e., jobs and low income housing."

In some ways, it was easier to be hard up before Downtown went uptown. If nothing else, men could sleep in the derelict Union Station and families could afford the pre-gentrification rent.

"[Homeless] people will say, 'If they're building these new and beautiful buildings, why can't they house the homeless?' They're upset about it and I don't blame them. Most of us are one paycheck away from being homeless."

Much is being done about homelessness by City Hall, the agencies, and the corporations. But it figures to be a while before, as Judith Watt puts it, "we've dealt ourselves out of business."

This winter is as far ahead as Angel and Anne Farringer are looking. She has the option of skipping it and taking a pay raise, but she's staying.

"I've kind of come full circle," she says. "I don't need a great yuppie lifestyle. I'm like the people on the street, who just want to have dignity, some friendships, a chance to go your way."

Metro Mixing

Its doors have just hissed shut, but the bus hasn't left the curb yet. Standard etiquette would appear to be on the side of the would-be passenger, a gangly middle-aged man in sore need of a shave and a change of clothes.

With the panache of a stockbroker hailing a cab, he gives the double doors a couple of sharp slaps and turns aside to await the response.

The response is no response. The driver, a billowing man with a billowing beard, throws the wise guy a long look through mirrored sunglasses and then pulls away from the curb.

Waving and cursing, disbelieving, the shabby fellow follows at a near-run, catching up when the bus has to stop for traffic a few yards up the street. He pounds on the doors again. Tough luck. Goodbye.

Shouting profanities, he storms through the Downtown bus stop crowd and into the Metro waiting station to pursue the matter. Evidently he gets no satisfaction, because he emerges a few minutes later, yelling and swearing and pointing at whoever is showing him the door.

He is left, finally, to find a section of storefront to lean against and wait for the next bus, alone in his stew. He could have worse problems, and even if he did, who around here would care?

The bus stop is a funny animal—a scene of easy camaraderie and cold distances all at the same time.

The high school kids, a fluid fashion revue of leather and

denim and male earrings and iridescent sweatshirts and large framed shades, are at home here. They argue, laugh, smoke, slap hands with passersby they may or may not know, appraise members of the opposite sex, tease (or is it taunt?) each other and total strangers, and even cruise to other bus stops and back again.

Other bus riders, for the most part, are separated. Separated from each other and especially from all the young dudes. Separated by a few feet of sidewalk, separated by race, sex, age and plain old city caution. They speak not, neither do they smile.

A frail old woman with a cane—she and it are like two sticks in a slow-motion stampede—stands sentry at the curb, scrutinizing the marquee of each stopping bus until the 31-Greenwood finally arrives.

The problem is, this is not its stop. It only slows for traffic, and she hobbles into the street after it, alternately planting and waving her cane.

After a long, level, what's-the-matter-lady-can't-you-read pause, the driver parts the doors and she hauls herself aboard, nearly toppling backward. No one moves to assist.

Nor does anyone heed the elderly couple, hatted and high-heeled and necktied in their threadbare best, who walk by with copies of *Awake* and *The Watchtower* displayed against their chests for sale. Nobody's buying, and they, their hopes for saving souls reserved for other times and places, chat with each other and keep going.

For all the uneasiness and aloneness felt by those outside the noisy youth crowd, the bus stop is a comfortable enough spot to spend a small piece of a sunny spring afternoon.

Until the air raids start, anyway.

Out of the east comes a short, shuffling guy wearing a '50s-style baggy black suit and a T-shirt, hugging a valise-sized radio that is detonating with some kind of rap song. Though he stares straight ahead, someone in the knot of kids works one of his hands free for a finger-shake and somehow conversation ensues.

The concussion of the boom box is physically painful. Its use is an act of astounding aggression made all the worse by the toleration it receives. But the people who don't like it are going to be gone in 10 minutes, or 15, and right now they are keeping cool and thanking God for the 10-English, the 13-West 10th, or the 18-North Meridian, comin' for to carry us home.

Jarheads' Refuge

If ever a book could be judged by its cover, this is it.

In its previous life, it was a washed-out storefront in the aging Fountain Square commercial district, a wooden pillbox with flat, stingy windows that made customers feel unwelcome as thieves.

Today, it is a riotous facade of bright blue and red and yellow, sporting a lighted sign that welcomes anyone who can show a certain simple qualification.

"Once a Marine, Always a Marine," the red letters say.

It takes permission or a passkey to enter the Indianapolis headquarters of the Marine Corps League, but there's nothing stuffy about this exclusive club. The outside was painted in the familiar Marine dress uniform colors, and the standing joke among those inside is that the joint ended up looking like a Chinese shrine.

Except for the framed map of Indochina tacked to a pillar, the inner sanctum is pure American. A braided Star-Spangled Banner and giant replicas of campaign medals dominate the walls. An L-shaped bar with Marine Corps decals on its cooler doors dominates the floor space. Neat red plates with yellow letters identify the "Galley" and the "Heads." Cigarette smoke and hearty male laughter fill the air.

It's a cold Saturday night just this side of winter, and the congressionally chartered organization has just installed its new officers. Counting 82-year-old Charles Crumbo, who saw action in the Banana Campaign in Haiti in 1917–18 and later served in World War II, every war since the Spanish-American is represented. The mood is high, and Don Myers is holding court.

". . . So here I am, trying to climb that goddamn cliff, and I've got my whole patrol strung out behind me, and of course, the gooks were good at that, right away they closed off . . ."

Retired Staff Sgt. Don Myers, USMC, was a professional soldier nearly two decades before they carried him home from Vietnam in 1969. He is the most decorated Hoosier Marine from that war. Prematurely gray and powerfully voiced, wearing a maroon sports coat with a nameplate on the pocket, he could pass for a state legislator at a campaign stop.

"Vietnam finally did me in. I went through Korea without getting wounded and I was wounded five times in Vietnam. I joke about it now—seems like every time I stood up, somebody shot me. I was beginning to think they had a personal grudge."

His pretty, dark-haired wife listens to the line for the umpteenth time and rolls her eyes at the laughter it sets off. Dorothy and Don met during the Vietnam War and were married while he was recuperating from that last hit. Together, they help nurture the fledgling chapter of the Marine Corps League, which is both a service organization and a place where the "jarheads," as Marines affectionately call other Marines, can draw close and tell their sea stories.

Around and around the bar, they tell them. Horror stories, some of them, but diluted to mere entertainment by the alcohol and the years.

Fred Chastain remembers the sergeant bound for Korea who bade farewell to his girlfriend by saying, "So long, slut. See ya when the war's over." He didn't make good on the pledge; he was killed in the landing. "Hard core," Chastain says.

Soft, choked laughter follows. Then someone else's recollection. Then someone else's. Eventually, it comes around to Dorothy Myers; or, more precisely, she finds a lull and decides to fill it.

She asks whether anyone saw that television documentary about the Vietnam veteran who confessed to his wife that he had stuffed live grenades down prisoners' shirts. She could not live with him and that knowledge, and he could not live with her rejection. He killed himself.

What would you say to a woman who has gone through that? Dorothy asks.

Except for the twanging of a country music show on the TV above the bar, the Marine Corps League falls quiet. The men around Mrs. Myers lower their eyes and slowly shake their heads.

"There is no glory in war," her husband says.

Poll Position

Arriving at the Riverside Community Center in the golden noon hour of last Tuesday, the voters of Ward 6, Precinct 8, came about as close to royal treatment as a common citizen can in this republic.

Their march up the wide placard-lined sidewalk was interrupted by one courteous greeter after another — this one explaining the school board ballot, that one offering free advice on the Center Township trustee's race, that one dispensing literature with a how-do-you-do-sir and a thanks-for-stopping-by-ma'am.

Voters are special when voters are few. None made them feel more distinguished than Philip Washington, the official poll inspector, the boss man in the pinstriped vanilla suit with the Masonic pin on one lapel and the gold key to the city on the other.

Philip Washington — slender, goateed, bespectacled, elegant — could only wish he felt like he looked. Up since before dawn, running on Kools, coffee, and a couple of doughnuts, busy with two full-time jobs besides this, he was fighting the Big Fade. Tuesday's primary, he sighed, might be his last election.

The voters — all black, mostly elderly, the women wearing dresses and the men sporting brimmed hats — had no cause to suspect. Washington knew virtually all of them, having spent most of his 40 years in the Northwestside neighborhood and half of them as a poll inspector. Even if he was a Republican in an overwhelmingly Democratic precinct, nobody who came to his election place got cheated.

Not the lady with the snapshots from her son's high school

prom. Not the Democratic state senator, Julia M. Carson, who got a kiss on the cheek. Not the Democratic state representative, William A. Crawford, who got a how-are-ya-Bill. Not the white-haired gent with the cane, who scolded Washington about smoking.

"I'm afraid I might get fat," Washington protested.

"Worry about gettin' short," the old man countered. "Don't worry about gettin' fat. The people in Washington will take care of that."

Truth be told, Philip Washington didn't altogether disagree. He lost his political idealism back in the 1960s, when he was a Young Republican pounding doors for a mayoral candidate named Richard G. Lugar. No particular offense to Lugar, but it has been a long time since Washington has expected politicians to change the world, or his life.

"The political process is just a machine—a tool," he said. "If these people could see how people in other countries live . . ."

Washington saw, in the Army, in Europe. But his involvement in politics came long before that. His mother is Pearlina Lensey, the ward chairman, a small crisp woman of 62 who has been poll-working since age 18. Her son remembers sitting on the bench with Republican judges when he was a toddler, the twig being bent an odd (for blacks) direction.

If Republicans ever wrest the inner city away from Washington's Democratic friends, he believes, another generation will have to do it.

"I was glad to see them lower the voting age to 18 so the young people could get involved," he said, squinting at the knot of teenagers with their leaflets, their boom box, and their trickle of voters to welcome. "But they've had a lot of disillusionment."

Yes, disillusionment. And then another elderly couple, inching away from the community center in the brilliant sunshine, caught the inspector's eye. "Thank you very much for coming," he told them.

Minding the Store

Albert Profeta holds a fat red tube of bologna against the slicing machine, loosing a potent aroma that momentarily fills the back section of his tiny grocery store. He smiles and shakes his head as he gathers the falling circles of meat.

"It was two years ago," the proprietor tells a visitor. "I'm not about to forget that."

Nor does he lack for reminders of "that." Today, for example, his right leg is bothering him a little. As evidenced by the hole cut from the end of his shoe, it tends to swell sometimes. The surgeons, he explains, had to tie off a vein when they removed the bullet from his back.

"Oh, we've had some petty holdups, but nothing to worry about—until this thing. Why those guys did that I'll never know. There was no resistance."

It happened on November 26, 1981, the day before Thanksgiving. Albert Profeta and his son Larry were doing the weekly inventory in Profeta's Market at 1000 West 30th Street. Three men entered and demanded money. In the wild two hours that followed, during which police surrounded the building, one of the intruders shot Albert Profeta.

The holdup men are in prison now and Albert Profeta is back at work, seven days a week, at the business he established a month and a half after his discharge from the service in 1946. The shooting put him out of commission for the better part of three months while his son and his wife, Rebecca, ran the store.

But even then, he insists, he never considered joining the exodus of merchants from the inner city.

"No!" he says with that same smile, gesturing toward the crowded walls blazing with yellow bottles of Joy and blue cans of Spam and orange boxes of Wheaties. "I like it just the way it is. You can't believe the people who came to see me or sent me a card. People from back in the '50s! I've got boxes of cards. I guess I've got more friends than I though I had."

Albert Profeta is going on 61 and looks younger. His hair is still mostly black, his glasses are stylishly large-framed and his white apron and pocketful of pens give him a purposeful appearance. But he's very conscious of how many miles he has walked over the uneven floor at 30th and Rader streets.

He points to a cardboard sign, dated 1953, that he still displays near the meat section. "Turkey: 23 cents a pound," it says.

Next to the sign are two picture frames filled with wallet photos of black children—pupils from across the street at School 41, which closed in 1981.

In a folder behind the front counter, the proprietor keeps another collection of photos—black-and-whites taken outside the store in the late '40s. More School 41 pupils, all of them white. "I'd love to know what those kids are doing today," he says.

The son of a near-Southside vegetable purveyor, Albert Profeta is among the last of that breed of meatcutter-grocers who handled every facet of their businesses and came to know customers like family. In the racially transformed neighborhood, many of these customers are poor, elderly, and dying off. "They say the economy's getting better," Profeta remarks. "I don't see it. If it wasn't for food stamps, we wouldn't survive."

Profeta believes he may have the last market in Indianapolis that uses a coal-burning, trash-burning Warm Morning stove. That stove in the center of the store caused a near-panic two years ago when one of the robbers tossed a gun into it and the weapon started firing. Police, who had removed all the bandits from the store by that time, thought for a couple of days that they had a fourth suspect.

Profeta laughs about the incident. He laughs about a lot of things others wouldn't. "Life seems to get sweeter when you get older," he says.

At the counter up front, a young man wearing a plastic hair net waits to pay for two bags of Fritos and two bottles of red pop. Profeta heads up the aisle to give him a greeting.

"What say, Slick?"

House Calls

Soul music blasts from the sagging front porch at 9th and Blake streets as Laurence Longman's 1962 Ford Falcon creaks to a stop against the far curb.

The two young dudes and their woman friend in red shorts regard the middle-aged white man languidly as he marches toward them, clad in short-sleeved shirt and tie, clutching a fat black book.

They trade hellos as Longman breezes by and bounds up the gloomy, linoleum-covered staircase leading to a second floor flat. There, he gives three robust twists to the old-fashioned doorbell and waits for another elderly client to answer.

It's Tuesday. The insurance man's here.

For the past nine years, for scores of black folks living on streets like Blake and Bellefontaine and Yandes and Martindale, that trusted white man who comes around to collect a little cash or an occasional check against the threats of death and illness has been one L. J. Longman.

He's been in the insurance business 31 years, most of it selling "debit" policies in the inner cities of Detroit and Indianapolis, and he doesn't mind a bit that the high-powered real estate planners with their CLUs call his a dying breed.

"My dad always worked for a living and I like working with the working class people," Longman explains as he steers the Falcon through his chuckhole-pocked territory, waving to his clients on the porches and the sidewalks.

"It's made me a decent living, an average of $25,000 for

seven, eight, nine years, and I haven't killed myself doing it. The ordinary business never really interested me. For one thing, there's the competition. You have to wine and dine people and I'm not a winer and diner."

The 9th and Blake stop typifies Longman's brand of garrulous efficiency. He collects a monthly premium of $7.32 and rises to leave only seconds after taking a seat on the couch. There's nothing perfunctory about it. He kids the old man for missing their appointment last week because he was working in the election somehow.

"This is still the greatest place, don't you think so?" Longman booms, hand on his client's stooped shoulder. "No matter what the politicians do with it, it's still the greatest country in the world."

It must be, when a salesman with a wad of cash in his pocket and irreplaceable papers in his unlocked car can ply the high-crime areas of two major cities with no apparent fear.

"I might think differently if somebody put a gun to my head," Longman says, "I've never been robbed and I don't worry about it. I couldn't work down here if I was afraid. We've had a couple agents quit because of it. One got beat up pretty bad. The dope addicts, they're the ones you have trouble with."

Longman thinks he almost got held up once. Three men approached as he was getting into his car and he quickly pulled two $1 bills out of his pocket and thrust them forth.

"I said, 'I've been meaning to buy you guys a drink.' They took it and I took off. Good thing, too. I had $200 in the car."

A far more congenial kind of crime usually haunts the street corners and alleyways of Longman's sales district. It waves at him in the form of a red-haired woman in a slit skirt as he eases the car into a trash-strewn parking lot behind an apartment building on Illinois Street. He waves back.

"There's a pair of legs for you," he chuckles, as the woman resumes her conversation with three men sitting on the trunk of a Buick. "She's one of the hustlers. She's tried to put the move on me a couple of times."

Inside, Longman patiently explains to a defeated-looking woman in a housecoat how the policy she's buying for her brother will pay so much for the loss of an eye, both eyes, both limbs, life. "I've been doing all the talking," he says. "Any questions?" She has none. He invites her to read the policy over and he leaves the sad basement apartment, ribbing her about TV soap operas as he goes.

"That lady won't read the policy, and if she did, and didn't understand it, she wouldn't ask me. So, I take the time to explain it. They don't deal with a company, they deal with L. J. Longman, and if I treat them right, they'll tell others. That chain hasn't changed in 30 years."

Longman guesstimates that he may have the largest debit agency in Indiana today, but he didn't think he could sell insurance at all when he took a friend's invitation to join National Life and Accident Insurance Co. in 1948.

A high school graduate, recently out of the Army and more recently made jobless by the collapse of the auto company he worked for, he gave insurance a try because "I had a wife and two kids who had the bad habit of wanting to eat."

The insurance business he entered in his native Detroit was the only kind Longman knew. The insurance man was cast along the same lines as the milkman and the breadman. He came once a week to collect a nickel or a dime for a burial policy worth a couple hundred dollars, and marked you "Paid" in his binder.

Now, it's more like $8 a month for a $1,000 policy. Customers are documented by computer cards. Many pay by mail. For the others, the insurance man still comes calling and inflation is the only change.

From the beginning, Longman worked the black community, where life insurance rarely was even offered before the 1950s. His company, which acquired a black health insurance club early in the century, was a pioneer in selling both life and health insurance to blacks. To this day, Longman still carries clients who pay 25 cents a week for health insurance that will pay them $5 a week when they're laid up.

Longman learned well enough to win three promotions at National Life, the last of which brought him to Indianapolis in 1962 as assistant manager of the local office. After nine years of that, he scratched an itch to return to selling.

He asked for and received the sales area bounded by 21st Street on the north, Washington Street on the south, Senate Avenue on the west, and Martindale Avenue on the east. When he started, the premiums mailed to him and paid in person totaled $200 a week. Now, it's $2,500.

"I selected the Downtown area for several reasons," he recalls. "We never had an agent who was successful there while I was manager. It was open. I wanted the challenge. This office [at 971 North Delaware Street] is heated in the winter and air-conditioned in the summer."

Longman's broad, animated face takes on a conspiratorial look as he turns the Falcon up Indiana Avenue and reflects on his choice.

"You'd really be surprised at the opportunity that there is Downtown. There's money going here and people don't think there is. If I didn't have the experience I have and you said I could make $25,000 here selling insurance, I'd say you could buy this area for $25,000."

In its way, Longman's cheery capitalism reflects more faith in the inner city than any social worker has. In the same way, with the same candor, he's as critical of urban policy as any community organizer.

"They tear the housing out and they don't build anything in its place," he fumes, gesturing out the window toward the recurrent vacant landscapes. "East of College on Bellefontaine, Cornell, Carrollton—they tore it all out. It was an established community of homeowners. They've all moved away."

When they moved away, they stayed with the company, but

changed agents. Longman hates to think of the "fantastic business" he would have had if they hadn't been forced out. But those who stayed are good customers. They pay their premiums. In 31 years, Longman has received one bum check.

Keeping customers current means not pressuring them to buy in the first place and not selling them more than they can afford, he confides. It also means getting them used to regular collections—Mondays, Tuesdays, and the first and 16th of the month, when welfare and Social Security checks arrive.

"It would surprise you the number of people who are ready to buy because they don't have any insurance. If they're not sold on the need for it, they'll drop it as soon as the financial pinch comes."

Need can be very basic in Longman's territory.

One of his 13 stops this sunny day is an elderly woman's tattered living room, where framed photographs of two young servicemen stare across at an automobile tire leaning against the wall.

The woman isn't sure that she signed for the insurance on her great-grandson and great-granddaughter, but Longman explains that she did so 10 years ago. He remembers her daughter on Ruckle Street, whose two daughters in turn are the mothers of the two children. She nods, peering past him through murky glasses, gathering her thoughts, nervously smoothing her dress with her long thin hands.

Longman does not try to explain the intricacies of what is being done, but he takes care of the customer's request. She needs the meager cash value from the policies, but he also wants to keep them in force to pay funeral expenses for the children, who live with her. He shows her the three places to sign, and she does so, complaining that her eyes are too weak to make out the spaces where she's writing.

By the way, she asks: Can she get one of these policies that will pay for the young girl's college education? It's too late, Longman tells her—college is only six years away. Better she set a little aside in a savings account.

His voice still at its high, healthy volume, he bids her goodbye. Like many of his visits, it has been profitless. He calls it the service part of the job.

"To have sold that woman a $20-a-month college endowment would have been a disservice and her family would have been right to call me on it," he says later. "She just wants the $90 cash value and $1,000 to put the kids away when they die. Her Social Security check is spent as soon as she gets it—the phone bill, food, and it's gone."

Laurence Logan will retire a year from this July, leaving the area where he has become such an incongruous fixture. He'll be 55 then, he's been well taken care of by the company's pension plan, and he figures he can make a fair sum of money in the household repair business. The Falcon was inherited from his ailing mother, and she needs attention. He has a wife and four grown children to enjoy, and no intention of killing himself chasing $8 and $18 insurance premiums.

That doesn't mean he's delighted to see "Downtown" change insurance men.

"I thought, back some years ago, that maybe I should have gone into the casualty business—auto, homeowners, and that sort of thing. I suppose all agents do. You get more commission for sales than service. I'm glad I stuck with life insurance, with the working people. I wouldn't do anything different."

Market Days into Night

Joseph Bova stood at the dock of Wilcher Produce Co. and pointed east, toward New Jersey Street. A rumpled sky-blue golf hat crowned his leathery face.

Ahead of him, the tops of Downtown's proudest office buildings brooded over the rain-splattered sheet metal roofs of the Indianapolis Farmers Market. Behind him in the gloomy block building that houses Wilcher's huge inventory, the air was sweet with oranges and grapefruit and apples and yams.

"This is a landmark here," Bova said. "I remember Old Man Lilly used to eat right over there in a boarding house. I mean the old man, J. K. Lilly, the guy who started the place. He drove an electric car."

Joe Bova is 79 years old. He's been retired for years, but he still comes by the Farmers Market at New Jersey and South streets practically every day. So do a lot of old hands.

Bob O'Neil. Alfred Lynn. Dorrell McClain. Albert Davis. Alfred Lacomb. All kinds of 25- and 40- and 50-year veterans of produce peddling, working nowadays anywhere from full-time to here and there to not at all. They're at the Farmers Market because it's home; or at least, it's their answer to the Columbia Club.

"Without this market," said Tony Mansfield, who is 59 and has worked there 45 years, "it's not Indianapolis."

Some care a whole lot less about the recently announced plans by Eli Lilly and Co., the giant neighbor to the south, to buy the 61-year-old property in what used to be Little Italy and tear it down by early 1988.

When the cronies gathered around the cardboard-burning stove in Troy Bridgeman's storage depot one afternoon last week, Lilly took the beating any rich corporation ought to expect.

But whether the Farmers Market, in its present form, deserves to stay was another matter.

Bridgeman, one of three year-round purveyors still on the premises, is 70 years old and has been around since 1938. He's just this side of retired. "All I need," he said, "is a loafing place. This costs me $243 a month. Most months I make enough to pay it. Sometimes I have to go into my [railroad] pension."

Troy's son, Stanley, who does most of the work nowadays, agrees they can move their tomatoes just fine without paying $243 a month for what amounts to an elevated garage.

The losers, Stanley said, will be consumers, who will find more pricing power concentrated in the hands of the larger wholesalers who left the Farmers Market years ago. Consumers, and the farmers and commission men from southern Indiana, Ohio, and Illinois who have brought their watermelons and cantaloupes and such to the Farmers Market through the years.

Growers have dwindled in number, but accommodating them remains a big job. Larry and Betty Wilcher, whose son Danny owns Wilcher's Produce, laughed at the notion that the City Market might take up the slack. The Wilchers do $1.5 million in business a year—from 40 tons of sweet potatoes to 10,000 Christmas trees.

"What goes through here in one day," Larry said, watching a forklift feed one of the company's red 10-wheel trucks, "you couldn't even put in the City Market."

The Wilchers, who've been around since the 1950s, insisted they aren't worried for themselves and aren't wedded to the location. They'd like to see a new Farmers Market in a better neighborhood, one where proprietors didn't have to worry about finding winos sleeping in the trash bins.

"It makes no difference to us," Larry said. "We'll find a place. But a lot of people are going to be put out of work."

Everybody around the market has advice for Lilly. Buy the market, fix it up, charge rent. Give jobs to some of the people it will displace. Give the handful of full-time tenants, and the small retail standholders who use the open areas in the warm months, a couple of years' notice before they have to move.

No one has more advice for Lilly than John Arnold, Betty Wilcher's brother. No one is more fatalistic, either. "There ain't no such thing as the little fella," he said, sipping coffee on the cold, aromatic dock.

John Arnold is 59. He was 17 when he first loaded produce onto Joe Bova's horsedrawn wagon. Now, he could watch his son, Donald, hoist yams with a forklift on a rainy day, a day that had a number on it.

"We have hundreds of old-timers," he said. "I don't know where they'll go. This is like home. I've seen hundreds and hundreds of people here. Thousands. I've seen 'em die here."

Kids on the Edge

Richard pads into the orange-and-yellow courtroom a few steps behind his mother, glancing about like a schoolboy who's just been caught throwing a spitball.

He wears a soiled red windbreaker and the basic uniform of the delinquency case — jeans and basketball shoes.

Dark and fine-featured, Richard looks like a 10-year-old and displays a 10-year-old's indifference to the man in the black robe peering down at him over a sheaf of legal papers.

But this little person is no child. Although his head barely clears the table as he slouches in a padded chair facing the judge, he is much older than 10 and no stranger to Juvenile Court.

Richard is about to be expelled from junior high school for slugging classmates, kicking an assistant principal, and assorted other violations. He comes before Judge Valan R. Boring today for a different offense, to wit, "Criminal conversion of a Sony Walkman stereo."

"Is all this true?" the judge asks him, thumbing through the school conduct reports as though they were transcripts of the Nixon tapes.

Richard doesn't speak at first, doesn't move. His fingers are at his mouth. Finally, he mumbles, "Not all."

"What part of it is true?" the judge demands.

Another long silence, broken by the judge. "It's all true, isn't it?"

"Yes."

Boring turns his narrowed eyes to Mom, who sits rigid and remote beside her son.

"I've tried my best to talk to him," she sighs. "I've done everything I could do . . . "

"The court will take the disposition under advisement until the 24th of November," the judge finally says. "He can be prepared to spend the Thanksgiving holiday in the detention center."

Silently, one behind the other, mother and son take their leave.

Richard is one of more than 4,000 delinquency cases that Boring and his three referees will have handled this year. By the end of some days, they seem to run together—a river of sneakers, shaggy hair, bad complexions, rock concert T-shirts and half-paralyzed parents.

That's a false impression, strictly speaking. The severity of offenses varies, and so do the backgrounds of the kids. Occasionally, a youth's father, not just one of the lawyers, wears a tailored suit and shined shoes into Boring's Easter-colored courtroom.

But in Boring's eight years in the most difficult of judgeships, the diminutive former deputy prosecutor has not been meting out justice to his peer group. The building at 25th Street and Keystone Avenue is a place where you have to be careful where you leave your coat, careful that your instructions are understood, careful that your hopes don't rise too high.

"You've got the do-gooders on the one hand telling you to smack them on the wrist, and the hard-liners on the other telling you to lock 'em all up," Boring tells a visitor. "Your only reward is to head some of them off at the pass so they don't end up Downtown some day."

Boring's reputation for sternness and fairness has kept the do-gooders and hard-liners pretty much at bay. In a typical afternoon, he sends this kid to the Indiana School for Boys, orders that one to shovel snow to pay his court costs, and tells another that he's free to go but had better bring his toothbrush if he shows up again.

The juveniles and their parents embrace, weep, protest, or simply turn and go. Many, no doubt, never learn the judge's name.

At the end of a day, when he drives away from the crime-ridden neighborhood surrounding the Juvenile Center, Boring wonders what will happen to some of them. What will happen to Richard, who calls his teachers "motherfuckers," and Deanna, who is supposed to join Alcoholics Anonymous, and Jerry, who assaulted a policeman?

What will happen to Robert?

Robert is a dark, burly 17-year-old who was found guilty of punching a retarded boy and trying to rob him. Boring sent him away with his mother to await sentencing, but Robert blew his chance for freedom on his way out of the courtroom. He threatened a witness.

Having ordered him brought back, Boring informs Robert he will be going, not home, but straight to the detention center. He is instructed to turn in his coat and wallet.

Furious, the tackle-sized youth tears off the jacket and flings it on the table in front of him. Immediately, he is surrounded by the bailiff and three policemen, then spread-eagled against the bright yellow wall and frisked. Within a minute or two, he is gone.

"I'm sorry, Mom," the judge says.

"That's all right," she replies. And with her son's stocking cap and shabby black coat in either hand, she hurries toward the door.

Playing the Numbers

SQB *6/1* . . . SYM *4/6* . . . GTE *40/7* . . .

Tirelessly, indifferently, the orange stream of stock market intelligence flows across the wall, disappearing and reappearing like old, old memories.

It's a slightly down market so far this afternoon, and that normally would mean a light turnout of board-watchers. Yet, all six spectators' chairs in this Downtown brokerage company are occupied, and a couple of other walk-ins are tapping at the video-display terminal on the counter as well.

Most of the people here are regulars. They come three, four, five times a week, sometimes for an hour and sometimes for most of the day. Sometimes they talk business and sometimes they just talk.

"You making any money, Clarence?" Manuel asks, easing into a second-row seat without removing his trench coat. Manuel is a lanky man with fine white hair and a voice like a baritone sax.

"I'm not trying to make any money," his friend replies.

"Aw, you make money whether you're trying or not."

Clarence laughs with everybody else. It's true, and he's proud of it. A pixyish fellow in a gray tweed suit and neat feathered fedora, he's 95 years old and claims to have bought his first stock in 1910—RCA for $4.50 a share. It's worth 10 times that now, and he's not selling.

Selling is something Clarence has almost never done. He's

bought enough to make $5 million in the market, he says, and his friends vouch for that.

SWX 6/4 . . . GE 9/5 . . . XON 50/2 . . .

Clarence comes here just about every day to watch his money. "It gives me something to do to kill the time," he says. He ran an antique store for 45 years for the same reason— something to do. "This," he says, waving toward the orange numbers and letters, "is where I made the money."

When Clarence was young, the fruits of his shrewd low buys were displayed on giant chalkboards with stepladders for the busy secretaries who read the ticker tapes.

The money meant a lot then. It took him all around the world and made him his own man. Now he comes down to the board for the same principal reason Manuel and Frances and Ray and the other retirees hang around here.

"People who watch the board live longer than other people," Ray submits. "It's better than just sitting around the house."

MOB 9/1 . . . GTE 40/7 . . . TXO 7/6 . . .

The conversation ricochets around, from the arcane numerology of the stock market to the competence of Ronald Reagan to the woes of the Indiana Pacers. Watchers ask whether anyone plans to stay 'til the 4 p.m. closing and see if there's a rally. Not today, most say.

Manuel asks about Paul, who was here earlier this afternoon. Paul's eye surgery didn't seem to do him any good. Ray and Clarence tell him. A successful cornea implant is a lot to expect when you're in the neighborhood of 90.

"Twenty-one years old again we won't be," Manuel reminds Clarence in his wonderful deep voice. "None of us, huh? After a certain point, you just go down."

Clarence, the oldest of them all, watches the orange numbers and letters appear and disappear. His copy of *The Wall Street Journal* rests in his lap. He turns to a newcomer in the crowd, someone who admits to absolute ignorance of the stock market.

"Buy some Ford stock," he tells him, brown eyes twinkling

behind his glasses. "It's low right now. Buy 10 shares. Get your feet wet!"

He throws back his head and laughs. When he was a kid, Clarence probably was the first of his gang to leap off the high dive.

TET 3/1 . . . GSU 4/1 . . . BMY 7/7 . . .

Hard Bargains at the Stockyards

Puzzled and angry, the early arrivals thrust their wet, searching snouts around the every-changing labyrinth of steel gates and send up their protests in clouds of steam.

The thousand or so hogs give off a deep, satisfying vibrato as they huddle and hop to the handlers' whips, but the 600 head of cattle trumpet so noisily that the buyers and sellers sometimes must dicker at a shout.

It is one of the coldest mornings of the year at the Indianapolis Stockyards, but the men who shiver in layers of sweatshirts take consolation when they consider the warm-weather potential of the manure and dust under this four-acre roof.

"This is the only million-dollar business in the world that's all verbal," says Mug Williams, a square-faced fellow with a quick smile. "There's no contract, nothing's written down. A man's word is his bond. It has to be or he won't last in the business. I've only been here 34 years. They ain't felt me out yet."

Williams is engaged in private treaty dealing, one of two ways in which cattle, hogs, and sheep are marketed at the stockyards. It entails a series of discreet caucuses between individual buyers and sellers, leading to settlement on the best price each side can obtain.

The other method, preferred by management of the stockyards because it establishes more competitive prices, is the wide-open auction. Today, about 1,000 head of cattle will be shuttled, shoved, whipped, and whistled through this process conducted in a small amphitheater reached by catwalk above the clamorous pens.

"This one's plumb fat, folks," Bruce Haley croons from his perch facing the theater seats as a sleek brown heifer emerges through a set of double doors to the fanfare of the seller's whip.

"N-o-o-o-o-w, gimmethirtydollarthirtydollarthirtydollar AND . . . Twentyfive! Thirtytwentyfivetwentyfivetwentyfive FIFTY! Thirtyfiftyfiftyfifty . . ."

As he sprays the room with his nasal machine-gun of a voice, Haley is catching slight gestures—a pointed finger here, a lifted scorecard there—and translating them into bids.

Grinning beneath his white cowboy hat, he also slings wisecracks at the slack faces, scolds those whose attention drifts away, and evaluates the doomed animals wandering across the straw-covered scale that serves as the stage.

The auctioneer doesn't have to be a livestock expert, but he has to know enough at a glance to start the bidding at a fair level. Typically, he will take less than half a minute to move a piece or group of livestock from entry to exit—barring such eventualities as an uncooperative bull that may send the salesman on the floor, like a toreador, scurrying behind one of the thick safety cages.

Lou Wendling, a poker-faced professional buyer, plucks his day's catch from the steady stream and pencils numbers onto a fistful of tally sheets. His raised finger will generate thousands of dollars in bills for his employer. Because of a post-holiday glut on the market, he has to fight for every penny per pound.

Wendling calls on 30 years of experience, which have honed his eye for grades of cattle and fine-tuned his ability to discriminate between valuable weight and belly-water.

"You can check all around, from Lexington to Milwaukee; there's a lot of cattle being moved around this week," he says. "It'll dry up and cows will get higher again. It's supply and demand. Supply and demand."

Like everybody else out there, Wendling would like to see

supply and demand work a little better. Neither buyers nor sellers are happy with the prices they strain to reach, and they don't think supermarkets are suffering along with them. So they kind of pull together, for all their hard bargaining in the pit.

"We yell and cuss at each other," say Bob Drake, a buyer following in the footsteps of his father and grandfather. "Then we go back to the house and we're friends again."

Names

The Great Wilno

Peru, Ind.—In this town of sawdust dreams, where grammar school children and their athletic big brothers and sisters pull on pastel leotards and conjure up the wonders of the Big Top for gasping crowds, the Human Cannonball lives and works.

W. W. Wilno, a tiny man of quick gestures and Prussian-accented wit, is 76 years old now. He took his last ride from the barrel of a gun in 1958, before most of the performers in the 20th Annual Peru Circus City Festival were born.

Their parents and grandparents remember him—a helmeted, leather-clad self-guided missile, blasting from a cloud of flash powder and rising, rising over the upturned faces of Lilliputian fairgoers, then curving and dropping through the wind and the screams into the safety of a net 200 feet away, from which he'd spring to the ground with hands raised in triumph.

Ladies and gentlemen, THE GRRRRREAT WILLLLLNO!

His was a household name in a Stupendous and Colossal era, and the circuses, fairs and amusement parks paid handsomely to splash it across their posters.

Willi Wilno vaulted the world's tallest Ferris wheel more than 40 years ago, and he remembers it all.

He also cannot forget the untold thousands of strangers he disappointed. He has lived with the belief that many came hoping to watch him die.

"Every night, I'd look at their faces," Wilno said. "Mildred [his wife] always would stand at the net and tell me if I wasn't hitting it right. One night at a carnival where I was performing, she overheard a woman say, 'I've been here every night and he hasn't hit that Ferris wheel yet.' "

Today, in a gaily transformed lumber warehouse known as the Peru Circus City Center, *The Grrrreat Willllno!* still is announced to paying crowds. But they no longer come to egg on the daredevil in his nightly flirtation with death. Their cheers are for a beloved teacher and his prize pupils.

Since he retired 21 years ago to his farm 14 miles east of here, Wilno has trained young Miami County circus enthusiasts to perform as aerialists in the town's nationally renowned three-ring festivals.

This year, the winnowing and coaching of the fresh-faced hopefuls began in April. From July 14 through 21, 11 energetic high school and college girls applied Wilno's lessons in nine warmly received shows.

Mildred was there every night, watching the pretty young entertainers spinning and swinging through their routines 30 feet overhead, but mostly watching Willi.

She wished he were relaxing with her in the bleachers, below the bandstand and the mock freak show posters, taking in the spectacle and guarding his fragile health. After more than 30 years with the man of no fear, worry remains her lot.

Wilno cares, but he can't help that. He has to make sure the customers see the best loop walk, cloud swing, balance bar and trapeze performances his girls can give them. As they smile their way across the ceiling, he's pacing, shouting, then stock still on one knee, his stare darting back and forth from the girls to the rigging men below on whom they depend.

Wilno knows that showtime is no time to relax. A friend of his was killed that way.

It happened one night in 1929, in Springfield, Massachusetts. The victim was Wilno's assistant, a fellow German named Henry Ackenhausen. He emerged from The Great Wilno's cannon with too little velocity and came up hideously short of the precious net, plunging to his death.

Ironically, Ackenhausen was substituting for Wilno, who was laid up with a broken collarbone and assorted other injuries suffered in a shot at Syracuse, New York, a few days earlier. Wilno had made it to the net, but barely and sloppily—and at 100 miles an hour, that's not good enough.

The loss of his friend and the worst injury of his career came during Wilno's first year in America and first year as a cannon artist. He thought about quitting and decided it wasn't the logical thing to do.

"I had no fear, because I knew why it happened," Wilno said. "The police came to investigate and asked me if something was wrong with the cannon. I had checked it. It was in working order. I offered to go back in the cannon right then and show them it worked perfectly. They told me that wasn't necessary."

Wilno concluded the fault was Ackenhausen's. He was relaxed, not rigid, at the moment the cannon was fired. "There's nothing to push when you do that. You come out like a piece of paper."

Wilno also believes his own accident may have contributed to Ackenhausen's by weighing on his assistant's mind. In his business, it is axiomatic that disaster comes to those who think about it.

As it turned out, the tragedy catalyzed Wilno's career. Newspapers throughout the United States and Europe trumpeted the incident—at first reporting that it was The Great Wilno who had been killed. The bonanza of free publicity swelled the crowds and won Wilno a contract with the then-great Hagenbeck-Wallace Circus, based in Peru.

In 1932, Wilno left the circus world forever. He scrapped the artillery gun he had brought from Germany, built a new 25-foot cannon, and walked off to work independently at carnivals, fairs, and amusement parks. He gladly traded the glamour of the Big Top for less travel, better pay, and better working conditions.

"A lot of people enjoyed the circus life. I never did," he said. "They worked the performers too hard. Three shows a day and no extra pay. If they put on shows to make money and we risk our lives, we should get paid."

Like any sorcerer with his trade secrets, Wilno never will tell how the cannon worked, how it flung a man skyward while creating the illusion he had been catapulted by an explosive charge. "There was no spring" is all he'll say.

It must be quite a piece of machinery. It fired The Great Wilno 60 feet into the air over the world's tallest Ferris wheel during the New York World's Fair in 1936. He sold it to a circus in Spain when he retired, and as far as he knows it's still in operation.

One wouldn't expect less from the hands of a German craftsman.

W. W. Wilno, born Otto Willi Wildrick in Dresden in 1903, was an 18-year-old Berlin watchmaker when he proclaimed to his parents one day in 1922 that he was not cut out for such a quiet life. He joined a three-member acrobatic troupe owned by a man named Erwin Welson, practiced three months, and gave his first public performance in Berlin in April of that same year.

For a product of the great German gymnastics clubs, he says, it was a piece of strudel.

Wilno played with Welson four years and performed with a trapeze troupe another year before striking out on his own. He developed a high pole act.

"You'd take an actual tree, usually oak, and plant it in the ground about three feet deep. Then you'd put another tree on top of it with two clamps so you could really swing. They'd hear the cracking noise as you swung back and forth, almost to the ground. They'd really scream!"

Later, Wilno switched to a cloud swing act for a while. "Then I hit big business," he said. "I built a cannon."

People had been shot out of cannons as entertainment since before Wilno was born, but there were few practitioners at any given time. Using what experience was available, plus his own mechanical and mathematical skills, Wilno made his gun and moved to America.

He knew little English and the world was on the verge of a depression, but there's little time to worry about those details when you're going to work every day to be shot.

Wilno describes the ear-splitting, terrifying process as matter-of-factly as a baseball pitcher explaining how to throw a curve ball.

"You don't hear the explosion because your mind's a blank. You come out head first and you're completely numb until you hit the highest plane.

"Then your senses come back and you realize you must turn over. The only way you can land is flat on your back—perfectly flat. Every year after the season they had to take me to the hospital to put my arms back in place. I've had dislocations of both arms from landing with them free. The ligaments are still very loose to this day."

The day he realized he had lost the Olympic diver's continuity, the hair-trigger control of his slender, speeding body, Wilno decided to retire.

"I knew I had to give it up," he says simply. "Nothing lasts forever."

Doesn't he miss the days of the big shows, of sharing the pantheon of traveling entertainment with the Karl Wallendas and the Emmett Kellys, of watching swarms of admirers plunk down their quarters and shillings and francs to watch him fly higher and farther than any other human rocket?

"No! I had all I want in my life—45 or 50 years in the business," Wilno answered. Then he waved toward the knots of giggling girls in tights and teenage boys on unicycles, waiting in the alley behind the circus center for their acts to be called.

"I'm still in the business," he said, "as you see."

Remembering Gus

Mitchell, Ind. —At night, with the four searchlights bathing its pale gray surface, the 44-foot monument to Virgil I. Grissom is an otherworldly sight, an eerie reminder to a small Indiana town of the reach of modern miracles.

Even on a cold, gray spitting afternoon, a 34-foot limestone replica of a Titan rocket, set atop 10-foot stone tablets, is a stunning object to contemplate.

Simple, sleek, and unique, it imparts a sense of completeness and transcendence, as if it fell from the heavens one day to replace a heroic favorite son taken before his time.

Don Caudell knows better. The proprietor of Holmes Hardware Inc. labored more than a dozen years to get a memorial erected in Mitchell to Gus Grissom, the fallen astronaut whom he had known since boyhood.

Money—particularly big money from out of town—proved hard to get. Plans for a grander monument had to be scaled down. Spray-painted obscenities had to be cleaned off the structure before it could be christened. No state or federal elected official graced the dedication with his presence.

All that was in the news in 1981, and has faded with the headlines that preceded it—Grissom's space flight with the original Mercury astronauts in 1961, his command of the first manned Gemini flight in 1965, his death with Roger Chafee and Ed White in the fire during their Apollo test in 1967.

As far as Caudell is concerned, it's just as well.

"It was a long time in coming," he says of the monument on

South Sixth Street, next to City Hall. "And probably it will have more meaning 25 years from now than it has now."

Grissom's home town is far from being the only Indiana site with a substantial memorial to him. There is, of course, Grissom Air Force Base in Peru; and three miles east of Mitchell is the Virgil I. Grissom State Memorial, which shares the administration building of Spring Mill State Park.

Caudell had a hand in the Spring Mill one, too. He suggested it to state officials and the Indiana congressional delegation during his trip to Washington for Grissom's burial in Arlington National Cemetery.

The austere, gray Gemini capsule that Grissom nicknamed The Unsinkable Molly Brown dominates the exhibit, which features a space suit and other artifacts, an audiovisual presentation, and a floor-to-ceiling montage.

Billy Carlisle, manager of the park, directs a visitor's attention to small holes in group photos of Grissom's grade school and high school classes. The holes are where the astronaut's face should be.

"People lovingly wore him out here," Carlisle says. "I guess they want to feel the kinship."

The guest registers at the park and at City Hall show the kinship is felt far beyond Mitchell, even beyond the United States. That is gratifying to Don Caudell, who remembers Gus Grissom as a kid without connections who worked his way to the stars and then found politicians lined up to get their pictures taken with him.

The big shots, for the most part, haven't seen the monument on Sixth Street. But Gus Grissom's parents, Dennis and Cecile, can see the glowing top from their house a few blocks away.

"Mr. Grissom told me, 'I don't go to bed at night that I don't go out and look at that,' " Caudell says. "That's worth something."

Driving Lotus Dickey

Paoli, Ind. — Two miles off the highway on a gravel stretch of roller coaster called Grease Gravy Road, wood smoke and string music pour forth from a one-room log cabin older than the century.

Lotus Dickey, who'll turn 76 this Christmas season of 1987, is at the kitchen table, under the bare ceiling bulb, singing one of his many original compositions in a brittle but bravely rangy voice reminiscent of Doc Watson's. His thick workman/farmer fingers ply the 20-some-year-old Maggini violin fretfully, as though it were a lamb he was trying to examine. His moccasined right foot taps in time.

> Got someone I'm wild about
> Couldn't be no sweeter
> You'll agree there ain't no doubt
> If you could only meet 'er . . .

"I play that old-time, driving-style fiddle," he says, lest there be doubt. "They love it, especially in the South. They hoot and holler."

They also speak his name, in hushed tones, in the Midwest and on both coasts. Folk music aficionados, of which there are many in southern Indiana, revere Lotus Dickey of Orange County as a fiddler and composer in the "traditional" or "hill" or "old-timey" genre.

Dickey, whose influences range from the Bible to Irving Berlin to the Grand Ole Opry, doesn't have a clear label to slap on himself. He does have a clear, though modest, ambition: He'd like to make an album of his work.

"If you're gonna have something, it's not worth anything just hidin' back in the bushes," he says in his luxurious drawl. "At my age, it's a little foolish, I guess. I started awful late in this."

That depends. Lotus Dickey started his musical life with church songs before he could walk and started playing the fiddle at age 8. It was an instrument owned by his older brother, Cyprian, who still lives up the road. "Nobody taught me," he says, "I just grew into it."

He played and sang and wrote songs all his life, making a living in a variety of other ways and rearing eight children without a wife. He composed "Indiana, My Home Sweet Home" while pouring concrete for Indiana University buildings in Bloomington.

"I don't know what made me do it," says this sturdy fellow with merry blue eyes and thinning gray hair, the image of a retired shop foreman more than a country bow scraper. "Just a flair, I guess. I had nothing particular in mind. As a grown man, I'd be walking behind a plow horse, making up songs. The birds probably tried to drown me out."

When he talks about a late start, Dickey means he was too busy surviving to make more than a hobby of music. That changed in 1981, when Dillon Bustin, a Bloomington (now Boston) folklorist, recruited him for a documentary film about older folks who were pursuing rustic lifestyles. A folk musician himself, Bustin already knew Dickey from fiddling contests throughout the state.

Bustin arranged for Dickey to play at a couple of state parks, then asked him, "How high do you want to go with this?" Dickey replied, "The sky's the limit," and ended up, against his better judgment, on an airplane.

That took him to a prestigious East Coast folk workshop and started a long skein of workshops, festivals, square dances, and school appearances, from here to Los Angeles to Chicago to

Washington, D.C. Along the way, Dickey has played and sung with some of the best in the business, including all three members of Metamora, the nationally renowned traditional music trio . based in Bloomington. On their own, many of those performers have done his songs.

Much as he's been "noised about," to use his term, Dickey regrets he's had to say no to lots of admirers seeking records and tapes. At last, he has a master tape of 14 of his original compositions and has a producer (if not yet the cash) for an album.

To the frustration of purists, perhaps, the music is a mixed bag. Dickey plays and sings every single one of them for a visitor on fiddle and guitar, from grave spirituals to love ballads to reels to blues. When he did his lowdown "Blue Monday" at the University of Chicago four years ago, "I got encores like it was an Elvis show," he chortles. "It wasn't my singin'. They just liked the song."

Brought up on hard work and the literal Bible, an occupant of this rough cabin for two-thirds of his life, Lotus Dickey comes by humility easily. "There's more important things than music," he says. "Can't worry about an album when there's people not gettin' enough to eat."

That's Lotus talking. Lotus playing is a wide-gapped grin and a tapping foot and dreamy lidded eyes, following those toiler's hands across the strings.

> Got someone I'm wild about
> Surely is a looker
> Gotta go and take her out
> Fore someone else's took 'er.

Air Garrison

Bloomington, Ind.—Forelock plunging to his eyebrows, bespectacled face mashed into an evil froggy squint, baggy beige shirt hanging from the long padded body that a crisp black tuxedo will grace in a couple hours, Garrison Keillor peers out into the vast gloom of the Indiana University Auditorium and says:

"It's like church."

And so it is—not just the stout, ornate building itself, but the air of reverence within it.

Keillor's own reverence was made clear when he scheduled the February 1992 performance by his American Radio Company here. He'd heard of Indiana University's music prowess back at the traveling show's home base of New York City. Finally here, he would be the object of veneration.

Any show business star tends to be the sun around which a room orbits; but this star is from a separate, smaller universe, without television or movies or DJs to magnify him or to hang him in the heavens to begin with.

He is in public radio, for pity's sake. He must have done it with talent—with intellect. Anyone savvy enough to be in his presence, even on assignment for a campus newspaper or a tiny FM station, must think himself part of an elect.

When the star turns downstage, with his foam cup of— What? Coffee? Evian? Booze?—and utters a sentence, it seems freighted like a parable not meant for the masses, who know only Kevin Costner and Madonna and other false messiahs and unblessed virgins.

Was he speaking to himself? we wonder. To the headset-wearers and clipboard-wavers swirling around him on stage? To us assorted pass-holders who speckle the calm lake of seats?

Was he joking? Does he expect a laugh?

What is appropriate behavior for a handful of eavesdroppers on a casual rehearsal for a show they'll soon see with a paying crowd of nearly 4,000?

A strange, stifling atmosphere descends. Because it seems tacky to applaud practice, Ivy Austin's pealing rendition of "Can't Get Indiana Off My Mind" echoes in hollow silence. A few barks of laughter greet the basso profundo duet by Garrison and Richard Muenz, a bit that will touch off a roar when American Radio Company airs live in a packed house:

The auditorium at Indiana U-u-u
Was built in '41
And designed by a man from Fort Wa-a-a-yne.
. . . Its capacity, 3,800 seats
O-r-r-r so-o-o-o.
It's for opera, grand opera
For immense ladies wearing big ho-r-r-rns.

"I sang so well you didn't recognize me," Garrison says.

"I'm missing a note, Maestro, but you'll fill me in," he says.

"This portion brought to you by the Kinsey Institute, America's leading authority on sex. . . . We're in the Yellow Pages under 'You Know What.' A guy goes out on a date . . .

"Is that romantic?" he chides the orchestra. "Strings swelling? Yes! Yes!"

Two, three hours of this. Shuffling papers, scratching out three minutes of dialogue in Lonesome Radio Theatre. Hovering over sly, petite Ivy Austin through a Hoagy Carmichael love song. When we hear it again in the real show, we'll have the satisfaction of the chosen few, but lose the joy of revelation.

Meanwhile, we wait, we of the press, and hope for our own audience—with the star who creates his own firmament.

As air time nears, we are paraded, single file, into the bowels of the old theater, into a room the width of a fruit cellar, set up with a table and microphone. A frazzled PR man keeps trying for Garrison, bringing Ivy and Richard and the rest of the cast to still our growling.

But Garrison is not snubbing us. Garrison is fussing. He is rewriting and rewriting, tinkering with the saga of Indiana Dan or the News from Lake Wobegon to the last minute.

"Sorry," the PR guy finally says. "His door's shut. There's some major writing going on."

We understand. We obey, marching back upstairs and through the auditorium. It is filling and buzzing, like church on Easter.

Never Enough Knight

It was one of those unifying media ordeals, like the death of a president or the rescue of a toddler from a well.

Male and female, young and old, sports lovers and normal people—during that spring of 1988, they would approach and ask the same question, often with hushed solemnity.

"Any word yet?"

"Have you heard anything?"

"Is Bobby gone, or what?"

I admit my complicity. When I picked up a newspaper, I'd skip the progress report on the missile treaty, the update on AIDS, the saga of Noriega.

I wanted to know if Bob Knight was going to New Mexico, as threatened. I wanted to know which airports he'd been seen in lately. I wanted to know exactly what he had refused to say, and to whom. And I had to look no farther than Page One.

The Knight watch. I was on it, and I wondered why. I don't have strong personal feelings about the guy. I'm not an Indiana University alumnus or an ardent IU basketball fan. I am convinced universities have better things to do than help Miller sell beer on weekends.

Still, there's this fascination with a coach called Coach. I share it, not just with the folks who plant red flags in their lawns whenever Bobby's teenage recruits sally forth; but with some heavyweights from far beyond the realm.

David *The Best and the Brightest* Halberstam claims to be a friend of Knight. John Feinstein of *The Washington Post* and Frank Deford of *Sports Illustrated* have played Boswell to his Samuel Johnson. An East Coast English professor whose name escapes me has extolled him in terms worthy of Philip of Macedonia—and nearly as obscure to the average sports junkie.

Knight, on various peoples' authority, is a genius, a boor, an adolescent, a father figure, a perfectionist, a tyrant, an egomaniac, a philanthropist, a raconteur, a reformer, a volcano, an oasis, a neanderthal, a Renaissance man, a peasant, a prince, and the northeast end of a Hoosier headed southwest.

Maybe they're all true. Without doubt, he's a successful coach and—unless he gives away a lot of money—a very rich man.

He doesn't act like other successful coaches or other rich men, and I suspect that's a key to his appeal. While the Digger Phelpses of the world stalk the sidelines in tailored suits and sculpted hairdos, Knight lets his belly protrude from a cheap sweater somebody's paying him to wear. He eats in the back room of a Bloomington diner and takes off fishing while sportswriters kneel in the snow outside his window.

A maverick. A rebel. A man who marches to the beat of his own drummer. But not a Thoreau-type rebel or an I. F. Stone–style maverick. Americans in large numbers never have revered individuals such as that, because they refuse to play the game. Knight plays it, wins it, delights or at least excites the masses, then tells them to kiss his northeast end if they have the slightest gripe with how he does it.

We eat it up. Muhammad Ali did the same thing to us, and we loved and hated him, even trotted out the hagiographers to call this madcap boxer a genius. Howard Cosell helped Ali do it, and we loved and hated that mediocre media creature as well.

Forget all the stuff about winning, chair-throwing, and especially integrity. Where is the integrity in a business that makes coaches millionaires for using free labor by ghetto kids? The bottom line is, we can't get enough of Bob Knight because we can't resist entertainers who insist they don't need us. Let's just admit it and—borrowing from his own immortal metaphor about rape—relax and enjoy the communal feast of Coach.

Let All Black Poets die as Trumpets,
And be buried in the dust of marching feet.
—For Black Poets Who Think of Suicide

Elegy to Etheridge

Black Americans won't be marching to the echo of Etheridge Knight's trumpet any more than whites throng to Gary Snyder's ecology drumbeat.

Poets who lead people are not poets on paper but poets on MTV and in the pulpit. The Reverend Jesse Jackson is America's leading poet, and Public Enemy drowns out all book-poets taken together.

Though he was not a churchgoer or a purchaser of rap music, his generosity and humility were such that Etheridge Knight ceded the territory of poetry to preaching and singing and, as he put it, "just plain people talkin'."

Better known among eminent white scholars than among the plain people he celebrated, Knight accepted his many honors largely for their pragmatic value and viewed poetry as a means of communion more than distinction.

"Poetry doesn't exist in this book," he told me a couple of years ago as he slapped his copy of *The Essential Etheridge Knight*, winner of the American Book Award. "Poetry belongs in people's ears.

"I got it figured, man. This is gonna disintegrate, you know what I mean? This paper. Now, if you're fortunate enough that a line or phrase from one of your poems can get into the language, then you might be around for a while."

Maybe a Knight seed will lodge and sprout perennially, in the manner of "far from the madding crowd" and "brave new world." If he had had an audience in the tens of thousands, the survival of "we free singers be, baby" or "he sees through stone" would be a cinch.

We owed him an audience that big, and owed ourselves the chance to hear him. Fearsome and lovely as his words were on the page, they were caged animals there, pacing to be freed by his bluesman's baritone.

It was cool to go to a Knight reading because this was a real dues-payer, a cat who had *been there*. Korean War, prison, heroin, alcohol, head-whippings, fleabags, love for family and women constantly asunder. Finally, there was the cancer that took his life in March of 1991, at age 61, after too many Pall Malls and cold nights.

Knight lived hard and could be hard on those close to him. Though his mother, Belzora Knight, and his dearest friend, the poet Elizabeth McKim, were at his side, his going into that good night of death was not gentle. But he was not the glaring, strutting militant. He was a lover, who seemed to know his uncaged words, along with his living, would make turmoil for lovers of words, and for lovers of him, to straighten up after.

Several hundred of us were left with a rare gift of grace one night in spring, 1990, at Butler University, when Knight closed a gritty political reading with "Circling the Daughter," written for his child, Tandiwe. The audience, mostly young, shot to its feet with a pounding ovation when he uttered the last lines in a cracking voice:

> Make the sound of your breathing
> A silver bell at midnight
> And the chilling wet of the morning dew . . .
> You break my heart with your beauty:
> Ooouu-baby-I-love-you.

Last fall, I saw Etheridge Knight for the final time. He introduced me to his son, Etheridge Bombata, who was in the Navy and maybe bound for the Persian Gulf.

"They let you raise them up," the poet said in front of his son, "then they take them and kill them."

They didn't kill the son, and Lord willing, they won't get the father either. If we love language for the life it gives, we have to believe his bristled, tender talk will bloom in the blown dust of prominent men's speeches.

Most Dangerous Wrestler

Dick "The Bruiser" Afflis was going about his business, cutting a man-size swath through the Roudebush Cold Spring Road Veterans Administration Hospital, when a staff sneak slapped a label on his tree-trunk chest.

It was done in the line of duty. It was National Salute to Hospitalized Veterans Day, and the whole throng of military brass, professional athletes, media personalities, political figures, and other VIPs who answered invitations to visit patients was issued name tags.

Dick Afflis took one look at his—"DICK THE BRUISER," it said—and peeled it from his royal blue fishnet T-shirt, growling. He ended up giving it to a paralyzed fellow named Bill, who, like most of the inhabitants of that hard little world, needed no help identifying this visitor.

"A lot of people don't like to come over here because they find it, oh, depressing," the Bruiser said, striding down a hallway with elbows out and basketball shoes toeing in, jock-style. "I like it. These guys relate to me"—snapping his fingers—"like that."

Dick Afflis is a celebrity who visits hospitals because he likes to, not out of noblesse oblige. A goal of the annual "salute" is to increase his tribe.

"This," said Roger Caron, an Indianapolis Colts lineman from Harvard who also made the hospital rounds, "is one guy's autograph I have to get."

It's a signature worth prizing. Though his closely held age is in the neighborhood of 60 and he's not getting Hulk Hogan's action, Dick's ruddy, square face and merry grimace exude vitality, and he remains a folk hero of his theatrical sport—whether or not he's a natural blond.

"The World's Most Dangerous Wrestler!" a young dude shouted through cupped hands when Dick burst into a therapy session for drug abusers. "The World's Most Dangerous Wrestler!"

"Save me a spot in here," Bruiser roared back. The group howled and applauded.

In the psychiatric unit, Dick was holding court about the tough guys of the past, Bobo Brazil and the Shire Brothers and the like, when a doctor escorted one particular patient forward.

Pale, shaggy, powerfully shy, the young man proceeded with an inching shuffle until he was nose-to-nose with Dick the Bruiser. He locked the great grappler in his gaze.

"You're bigger than me," he said.

"But you're better built," Dick barked back, seizing his shoulders. "You've got a better frame."

Smiling and staring, the patient rolled up his right sleeve and flexed his modest bicep. "Wow, take a look at that," Dick exclaimed.

It was time to break away, to see the two guys with the Bibles to be autographed and the others who clamored for his attention. As he turned, Dick touched the rapt young man on the forearm. His thick fingers were light as a priest's and the banter left his hoarse voice. "You take care," he said.

When the entourage of visitors departed the locked ward and glanced back through the reinforced window, the young man was there, watching. He put up his fists, and when Dick the Bruiser squared off too, he grinned enormously.

So did the World's Most Dangerous Wrestler.

Giving a Bluesman His Due

At 10:30 on a rainy morning, a gloom like late evening crowds James "Yank" Rachell's living room. Limp maroon curtains cover the two windows and most of the light comes from the television, on which Bob Eubanks is chirping questions about marital infidelity at quiz show contestants. The air is heavy with the smell of stew.

This is supposed to be an interview, but the 76-year-old man on the couch gives most of his attention to Bob Eubanks and to his two small great-grandchildren, whom he is irritably babysitting. The pleated, deep brown face opens only to chide the kids or answer specific questions. The celebrated voice, strong and seasoned as a blacksmith's bellows, sounds angry more than anything.

"The reason I don't do much talk," he says, "is people come and write you up and won't give you a quarter. I figure they must be gettin' something out of it or they wouldn't be doing it."

Yank Rachell has been written up a lot. He's the type feature writers love to discover. He's a legend, one of a dying breed—a black, Southern, country bluesman, playing it like the feature writer assumes it always was.

Better still, Rachell is a blues mandolin player. Hardly anybody plays blues on the mandolin. Rachell has done it since he bought one of the compact, plinkety instruments on impulse at age "eight or nine." He recorded his first album in 1929 and his latest, "Yank Rachell: Blues Mandolin Man," just this year on Blind Pig Records. He's lived in Indianapolis since 1957, but his music still arrives fresh from Brownsville, Tennessee.

"I've got my kind of way. I don't play like other people do. I got my own style. People will say, 'Can you play like B.B.?' and I'll say, 'Yeah, just put some string on it.' "

What he means is, he doesn't play chords like B. B. King and many others who sing and strum. He picks it, right along with the melody. Nobody taught him. Hardly anybody in a given audience knows exactly what he's doing. But they like it. In Canada, in Europe, all over this country, Yank Rachell's name is known.

At other times, in other genres of music, recognition has been accompanied by money. As we all know, it was the lot of bluesmen to part the seas for rock and soul without entering the promised land themselves.

Yank Rachell has lost count of the number of songs he has composed (he never writes them down). Some have become standards, and many have been recorded by the top names in the business—Taj Mahal, Big Joe Williams, Albert King. Presumably, Albert King doesn't sit across from Bob Eubanks on a worn-out couch with a bold little mouse circling his feet.

"Oh, yeah," Yank Rachell says. "I'd be rich if I had the money I had stolen from me. I'd be a millionaire. But you didn't know what you didn't know in those days. People'd take advantage of you."

If he had the time and the stomach for it, maybe he'd get a lawyer and fight for some of those old royalties, he says. For certain, he's past being flattered by "appreciators" of the blues who want to hear him talk, sing, and play for free. If he bought that, he could have an audience every weekend. For now, he's staying home.

"I ain't gonna play out there for nothing. I need something. I throwed away enough talent all my life. I'm too old for that."

Voting for Jesse

The first time Herman Bush voted for a non-socialist for president, he chose Franklin Delano Roosevelt.

Ask him what year that was and he replies: "Now you got me."

But he knows why he voted for FDR, and voted for him again and again.

"Roosevelt, the first thing he done, he told the rich man, 'If you don't open up your money, I'm gonna declare it all counterfeit.'

"And"—he chuckles and thumps his metal cane on the floor—"the money come out."

Born five years before the turn of the century, Herman Bush has voted in a lot of elections since he helped put the father of the New Deal into office. As do most of his fellow residents of the Mount Zion Geriatric Center on the predominantly black near-Northside, he has a built-in sense of history.

But when you ask him and his closest friends—like Mildred Sloan and Eugene Reed and Rose R. Anderson—to talk about elections, they keep coming back to two men:

Franklin D. Roosevelt, who gave them Social Security, and the Rev. Jesse L. Jackson, who gave them the opportunity to vote for a serious black contender for president of the United States.

The significance of Jesse Jackson's strong showing in the 1984 Decomcratic primary cannot be explained so much as felt. It defies the mathematics and quarrels by which presidential candidates normally are defined. It doesn't even have that much to do with Jackson's own merits and shortcomings.

To appreciate Jesse Jackson, meet Mildred Sloan, 77 years old, who lived in Columbus, Texas, when black people couldn't vote, much less seek office.

Did she vote for Jackson?

"Well, yes I did. He was a colored minister. I believe he has been in this world long enough to know the right things of God and the wrong things of man. I wanted him to be the first black man to be president."

Religion and race never have been separate for these elderly blacks, and politics can't operate independently of either. When Jesse Jackson paid a campaign visit to Mount Zion on April 20, he delivered a sermon as much as a speech.

Rose R. Anderson remembers that she wept as she listened in her wheelchair that day. The impassioned young minister reminded her of Dr. Martin Luther King Jr., another preacher who dared to rouse black people to move for social change.

Had he not been murdered, could King have become president?

"I don't think they would have allowed him to get that far. He would've been struck down. One thing that impressed us was that Rev. Jackson had the fortitude and the guts as a black man to step in the ring."

Her friends nod in unison as though the bright nursing home dining area in which they are assembled were a church and she were calling an amen.

White-haired, erect, her 77-year-old eyes flashing behind thick lenses, Rose Anderson goes on to confess her fear about Jesse Jackson. She is afraid "they" will stop him, too, by whatever means it takes.

"This is a racist country, whether we like to admit it or not. The handwriting is on the wall if we would just see it."

Yet, hope defies the bitterness and the meaner realities. It worked long before Jesse Jackson came. It brought these people through a Depression that was worse than the one white folks knew. And it flared when the absentee ballots were passed around at Mount Zion.

But a black president, not just a black candidate? Herman Bush and Rose Anderson say it will happen, but not in their lifetimes.

Eugene Reed isn't so sure about that. The 94-year-old "mountaineer from Paris, Kentucky," rears back in his wheelchair, folds his thin arms, and smiles like a guy with a secret.

"Yes, sir," he proclaims. "I think Jesus will let me live to see it."

Ryan and Friends

The sky against the awesome spires of Second Presbyterian Church was bright blue at 8:30 on Wednesday morning, April 11, 1990, but the wind was nasty and the worst was yet to come.

"I should have worn two pairs of socks," Nancy Fleek lamented, doing an involuntary impression of the Michael Jackson moonwalk in her spring sandals.

Already, she and her friend Charlene Wiley had been on the go for two hours. They'd caught the bus from their neighborhood on the Eastside and barely made the Downtown transfer to this Northside palace of worship where Ryan White would be sent to his rest.

"He would have laughed," Charlene said, "to see two girls running after the Metro bus to get here."

She spoke as if she knew him personally, though she had never met the frail teenager with the mirthful features who became an international champion for AIDS patients.

"In God's way, I think we're all his brothers and sisters," she said. And it wasn't just a ceremonial cliché; it was real familiarity, and so many others among the hundreds who came to say goodbye seemed to feel it as well.

"We've been with him ever since he first found out he had AIDS," Nancy Fleek said. "He had such courage in keeping up the fight. He didn't dwell on death. Anybody who can do that is real special.

Nancy shares a birthday with Ryan—December 6. She plays Nintendo, as he did. She considers herself his friend, like thousands of others who knew him only through television, newspapers, or letters.

Like Jay Jackson, just a few months older than Ryan at 19, who drove all night from Chattanooga, Tennessee, to see him Wednesday for the first time after writing him for many months.

Like white-haired Noma Goodman, who clutched a reporter's arm and said, "Ever since he got sick, the first thing I'd do was pick up the paper and see how he was doing."

Like Eric Lewis and Beth Lindsay, who stood in line for the morning visitation, clutching roses and fighting back tears. "He was such an inspiration," Lewis said. "I think he opened a lot of minds."

For some, the unmet friend did more than that.

Andy Wall and Philip Hinds arrived at Second Presbyterian Church with family members and friends, wearing buttons calling for tolerance for AIDS patients. They know AIDS firsthand.

"When I was first diagnosed, my doctor said to look around for inspiration," Wall said. "I did, and I saw Ryan."

Wall is 24 and was diagnosed in 1988. Hinds is 23 and was diagnosed in 1986. They have been friends since third grade. They get depressed. They have suffered bigotry. They wonder if some of the celebrities who drew a horde of photographers to Indianapolis really care about Ryan White or his anonymous survivors, those who live with an incurable and despised illness.

"Ryan has helped a lot," said Hinds, thin and pale in his black overcoat. "I don't think we'll find someone to carry his torch."

The early arrivals, the friends who came before Michael Jackson and Barbara Bush and most of the news media, got to see Ryan, decked out in denim jacket and mirror sunglasses under a soaring stained-glass image of the risen Christ.

But the afternoon funeral, unlike the morning visitation, filled the vast church quickly, leaving hundreds in the cold and intermittent rain with the waiting limousines, deprived of the chilling choir music and Elton John's simple song of tribute at the piano.

Nancy Fleek and Charlene Wiley, just about the earliest arrivals, failed to beat the rock concert-style crush at the church door and ended up soaked after all those hours.

"I almost got in," Nancy said matter-of-factly. "But I got shoved out. It could have been better organized."

She was still doing dance steps, this time trying to see who was in which departing car.

"Michael and Jeanne are in the first limo behind the hearse," Charlene told her excitedly.

Oh, Lord. Was it truly Michael Jackson, superstar, and Jeanne White, Ryan's mother, friends among friends?

"You can't see a thing through that tinted glass," Nancy said.

Games

The Princes of Pulling

Like an aroused beast from your worst nightmare, Big Ben Orange rips the flame-scented air of the Indiana Fairgrounds Coliseum with the unmuffled voice of five supercharged, fuel-injected, 427-cubic-inch Chevrolet truck engines.

In the sparsely filled grandstands, fans in blue jeans and flannel shirts and thermal vests and billed brand-name caps raise their fingers to their ears and hunker down. They have shuddered through two hours of the aural roller-coaster known as the Indy Super Pull, and the man most of them have been waiting for is finally at the starting line.

"Let's hear it for the Banter brothers," the P.A. man croons into the din. "How many think they can win this class, huh?"

A rhetorical question. He laughs as he asks it. The Banter brothers—Dave, the driver, from Warren, Indiana, and Ralph, the builder, of LaFontaine—all but own the 9,000-pound modified class.

The guys who've gone before them tonight, top qualifiers from all over the country, will end up fighting for third place, because when Dave gets done with Big Ben Orange, he'll jump onto Big Ben Blue, which carries six engines, and make it a double. Then he'll add and subtract some engines and come back for more loot in the 11,000-pound and 7,000-pound classes. The princes of pulling, the Banter brothers are, and the home crowd adores them.

BANTER FANS FROM WARREN ARE HERE, proclaims the only noncommercial banner in a pageant of RED MAN chewing tobacco and KENDALL motor oil and COUNTER systemic insecticide. "How many think they can make it two?" the P.A. man teases the rooting section.

A commanding, toe-to-toe sort of guy in conversation, Dave Banter takes on a Chaplinesque, what-have-I-gotten-myself-into look as he assumes his perch above and behind the five terrible motors and their 40 naked manifold pipes. The look isn't real; just the odd effect of squeezing an open, serene face into a black crash helmet until there's virtually nothing visible but eyes, nose, and mustache. An innocent spectator can gaze upon Dave Banter geared for battle and imagine himself atop that monster from hell.

Big Ben Orange, like Big Ben Blue, is essentially a bundle of engines with a frame to hold them, two little front tires to guide them and two tractor tires the size of whale udders to drive their thousands of horsepower into the ground.

This $80,000 conveyance is hitched to an equally awesome contraption known as a weight transfer machine, or "sled." The sled, with wheels and a tillerman, like a hook-and-ladder truck, carries the weight that the tractor pulls and moves the weight ever forward as the tractor labors, finally passing the point of leverage and leaving the tractor spinning impotently, its Leviathan tires spewing chunks of clay into the audience at 100 miles an hour.

Big Ben Orange will become the first puller of the night to reach the end of the course, the 243-foot mark, before the sled can exhaust the five howling Chevies. That's all there is; that's the grand slam home run of what the National Tractor Pullers Association calls "America's fastest growing motorsport." If it were not for the noise, maybe very few folks would care. But you have never heard anything, not even at the Indianapolis Motor Speedway, like this.

The roar of Dave's bristling dragon is almost painful in warmups; but once the green flag drops, the front tires lift and the mammoth sled begins to ease out of the chute, bubble lights flashing and advertising banners waving, the noise becomes un-bearable. Ears ring and throb even when they're covered. There is a sensation, watching the fat tires churn the packed surface as Dave grapples with the steering wheel, that the Coliseum is a gi-ant submarine and we're being depth-charged.

Unheard, the fans across the way are cheering, standing and pumping their arms as Big Ben Orange claws past the markers—50 feet, 100 feet, then an alarming swing to the right, so close to the course boundary that the tractor sends the 150 marker flying.

Still hauling like a locomotive at 200 feet, Big Ben Orange wriggles for that last grudging shred of leverage as it bears down on the checkered flag at about 230. At last, standing at a 45-degree angle to the ground and shrieking its defiance of the laws of nature, it burrows to a stop near the far wall.

A Full Pull, they call it, and the crowd is in silent ecstasy, still drowned out by the gasps by Big Ben Orange, but shouting their love for the man who vents its wrath. Dave Banter waves and then jogs back to the starting line, where Big Ben Blue, an-grier still, awaits.

Hoosier Italiano

Lou Caporale's ball looks good. Looks awful good. Think we're gonna like it. Think we're gonna love it.

Right down the middle it's coming, just the right speed, not too *forte*, not too *piano*, heading right for the bright orange *palino*, the target ball.

Hunched over in his follow-through, hands on knees, like a football coach on the sidelines (which he used to be), Lou glares at his shot all the way down. He knows the hard, two-pound soft-ball-sized sphere has to touch the *palino*, or darn near, to make this a point frame. "Come on!" he bellows. "Come on!"

Five other guys, his teammates, are helping it, too; pushing with their voices, guiding with their eyes, contorted with body English. Come on!

And it's coming. And it's coming. And . . .

Yes! He got it!

Kisser!

Mama ball!

Hoooooooooooooooo, yeah!

"Bravo!" Tony Maio shouts, arms upraised as if in a wedding dance. "Oh, Lou!"

"That," Carl La Mantia proclaims, "was a classic shot."

And this, Hoosiers, is bocce, the mixture of bowling and horseshoes and cigars and camaraderie that goes on a lot in big, ethnic cities but has only one known venue around here.

That venue is the country home of Phil DeFabis at Stone's Crossing in Johnson County. Phil, who is president of the Indianapolis Bocce Club, constructed the 90-by-30-foot clay court in 1975, moving the sport's only local site from Christian Park on near-East-side Indianapolis, where it had been the previous 10 years.

The area's Italian-Americans have moved as well over the past several decades, dispersing from the near-Eastside and near-Southside neighborhoods where guys like Lou and Tony and Carl and Phil grew up.

There's nothing ethnically exclusive about the bocce games they hold every Wednesday night in warm weather. There are plenty of honorary paisans to share the glory and needling — guys like Gene Kramer, Bill Huke, Lamar Updike.

At the same time, there's no mistaking where it came from. The little peg scoreboards are painted in the Italian national colors — red, white, and green. A ball that comes to a stop against the *palino* is a Mama ball or a Papa ball. Make that shot in the clutch, and you'll hear bravo!

Bocce, like veal scaloppine, is a taste of Italy for everybody. Phil DeFabis would like to expand its popularity. "Anybody can play the game, that's the beauty," he says.

Not just anybody can play like Phil, the club's defending champion from last year. He and Carl La Mantia have won the state tournament held every Labor Day weekend as part of the Little Italy Festival at Clinton. Trim, white-haired, an elegant senior presence on the court, Phil throws a bravo ball.

Besides court bocce, the grass version — forerunner of England's bowling on the green — is played at the DeFabis residence. The annual tournament last July 4 drew 56 competitors.

The Wednesday night affairs tend to be more relaxed.

Oh sure, the losers have to reach for their wallets. Expletives have been heard. Participants have stormed home without a good-bye. The tape measure has been whipped out to settle disputes over whose ball is nearest the *palino*. You ask for bocce, you get it spicy.

"You play this a couple of times, you get involved," Bill Huke says, stogie clenched in his wide smile. "It's a lot of fun. A lot of harassment."

Mayor of the Fair

The opening of the Marion County Fair was still a day away, but the midway already was swarming Wednesday afternoon. Their Jack Daniel's and Harley-Davidson T-shirts stripped away by the withering sun, the carnies were pushing hard to get the shoot-till-you-win booths nailed up and the Rock'n'Roll ride ready for the coming wave of toddlers, varsity studs, and giggling girls on parade.

"It's like setting up a whole town," Ed Coate said, leaning against the railing of the Dodgem Cars and quaffing a Pepsi, the paper cup muddy from his hard-worked hands. "We set it up here, and then it becomes your town. If you abuse it, we throw you out."

He said it, not with belligerence or bravado, but rather with an air of placid authority, like a multi-term mayor who has no need for glad-handing.

Ed Coate, ride foreman, is 25 years old and has not quite a junior high school education. As he spoke, he was covered with grease and dirt from the collar of his red knit shirt to the toenails in his thongs. His thick glasses were reinforced on both sides with duct tape, and his brown hair and sideburns were too long to pass executive muster. The college boys probably don't envy him, and you know, it's mutual.

"The travel—you're like an addict. Once you've gotten a taste of it, you just can't do without it."

Coate is in the minority nowadays—an "old carnie," not one of those come-and-go dilettantes they call "40-milers" in the trade. He has been abroad four times with the carnival and has seen most of the United States, sleeping in trailers and occasionally on the ground for at least nine months a year. Born to a carnie mother, he was on his first ride at 11 weeks and was running rides when he was 9 years old. At 15, he left his home in Michigan and never looked back.

"I can't read and write very good," he said, "but you don't really have to know how to read and write in this business. You have to know a lot of other things, though."

He gestured toward a tool-littered, half-finished multi-colored apparatus called The Twister—one of his setup responsibilities.

"You have to know wiring. You have to know wiring codes. You have to know hydraulics. . . . You know, when these amusement parks like Six Flags have accidents, it comes back on us. But what people don't realize is, these rides get inspected every time they're set up. No operator here would let anybody on a ride if he wasn't sure it was safe."

While he didn't come out and say it, Coate made it evident he wanted his listener to set this discourse on professionalism alongside the stereotype of the vagabond carnie. He and his wife, Donna, who sells tickets, make more than they would in 9-to-5 jobs, he said; and their 5-week-old daughter, Misty Dawn, doesn't lack for anything, the way they see it.

Still, it's not easy. Clad in a bright yellow sleeper and reposing in her mother's arms in the shade of the Dodgem's canopy, the black-haired baby was the image of health. But she was born with a serious liver ailment, and Mom and Dad must work constant medical care into their rolling schedule.

"We just take her papers around with us wherever we go," Coate explained. "She sees a different doctor in every town."

Home life, he said is not sacrificed for the carnival. But it is redefined.

"Carnival people are closer than most families. You might see us arguing and fighting, but it doesn't mean nothing. Once the fight is over, it's over. In this line of work, you couldn't make it if you didn't help each other out."

A moment later, the call for help came. Ed hustled over to the half-built Twister and Donna resumed walking the baby.

A few more breakdowns and setups, a few more states and new doctors, and they would be in Florida again for the winter. If they were lucky, they might get a winter tour and stay on the road all the way to the Bahamas. Then back to your town, or yours, in another spring.

Take on the Race, and It Wins

It occurred to me last Saturday, as I tried to cover the 500-Mile Race, that it really isn't possible.

The thing is too big, in too many ways, for any army of journalists to bring home.

There's no counting the people, no interviewing everybody who's important enough or crazy enough to deserve it, no conveying—not even on live television—the sensory undertow of its noise and odor and color and danger and flesh.

Most reports in the news media miss the sensation of the place entirely. Sportscasters in race driver suits croon clichés and promotions. Sportswriters exhaust their space with historical data—who won, how fast, for how much money. Feature writers like myself confront an elephant and settle for a detailed description of a trunk or a tail or a tusk. Depending on our mood and where we found a parking space, we might give you heroism or mirth or gluttony. No virtue or vice is missing in a crowd of this magnitude.

At other national sporting events, reporters are a bigger deal. Press credentials are like a Western diplomatic carte blanche in some desperate Third World country; the beggars part for your limousine. The "500" is too big for that, too thick with VIPs and their friends and relatives. Everybody, it sometimes seems, has a badge that allows unmolested entree, even to the edge of the volatile pits.

That's during the race. Before and after the race, this privileged horde can go into the pits, onto the track, wherever the cars are—posing alongside them for Uncle Joe's Instamatic and Cousin Fern's Canovision Battery Pack BP-E4 and Brother Bill's brand-new Nikon EM with the Porter Waggoner guitar strap. Protecting all that delicate, hugely expensive machinery from such a mob, well-behaved as it is, has to take luck.

Much else about the "500" is hard to understand, from the willingness of its neighbors to let their lawns be ruined for $5 per parked car to the unrelenting air-raid drone of a P.A. announcer exhorting us to "give him a nice round of applause." In an age when race cars are transported in semi-trailers that make my house look like a shack, these folksy traditions cling fast. Maybe there's a reason. What's depressing to some of us may be reassuring to others.

"Nothing ever changes around here," a reporter sighed as he watched the cooler-clutching crowd parade by at 8 o'clock in the morning. "Some of these people haven't missed a race in 40 years. They schedule their vacations around the '500.' "

I know. I've interviewed some of them. I've met serious fans, picnicker fans, and guys who like to get drunk by 7 a.m. and howl at a thousand women by dusk. None of them is representative, and all of them are.

Two things unite them, or come close: The start of the race and the finish. Thousands seek their own amusement for the couple of hours in between, but virtually everyone is alert to those first banshee shrieks of the engines, the kamikaze plunge of the pack into Turn One, and the climactic joy of a faceless survivor taking the checkered flag.

Even the pure thrills have to take their schmaltz dip. After surviving three hours of mortal danger, the winning driver is proffered along with his car toward the crowd on a large hydraulic lift, packed to the edge with crew members, officials, sponsors, interviewers—and bagpipers in kilts.

It's too much. Just too much. How in the world do you do it justice in the eyes and ears and glands of somebody who wasn't there?

Champions

Stevie Wonder wants to f-i-i-i-nd him a pl-a-a-a-ce in the sun, and so does Larry Sheets, who's got Stevie on his boom box in a far corner of the PAL Club gym. The wail from the tapedeck bathing him like warm sweat, Sheets bounces into his workout whipping a jump rope over and under his rubbery body and keeping his eyes fixed on a full-length mirror.

There are a half-dozen other guys here, thumping on the big bag, rapping on the speed bag, darting and dancing around the soiled canvas of the ring. But Larry Sheets is alone, all the same.

Snap. Snap. Snap. Got to find me a pl-a-a-a-ce . . . *Snap. Snap. Snap* . . . i-i-i-n the sun.

"They told me. 'There's no way this guy's just had two fights,' " Charlie Skelton says, recalling Sheets' last bout out of town. "I said, 'It's the truth. You can check his AAU card.' "

The red-haired coach laughs, marveling at the athlete's sudden development and at Sheets' own lack of astonishment at being so good so soon. A decidedly dangerous 178-pounder, the easygoing young man in ragged cutoff sweatpants may beat a living out of boxing some day.

If he does, it won't be just because he has harder hands or faster feet than somebody else. He'll also need a bigger heart and a smaller stomach than your average tough kid.

"The problem with most pro fighters in Indianapolis is they have to work for a living," says Skelton, who fought in the Air Force years ago and has a son in amateur boxing. "You try to work

8–10 hours a day and then train for a fight. It's rough. Training for a fight takes everything you've got."

For most of the 50-odd members of the PAL Club, the training itself will have to suffice. That and the cigar smoke and the sweet-onion smell of sweat and liniment that mark this place off as a hideout for men only.

As long as Colion "Champ" Chaney is in charge, everyone here, from the 10-year-olds to the 200-pound men, will be equal. He is the equalizer. Less than two months shy of his 60th birthday, Chaney will climb into the ring with any of his pupils—children, weekend athletes, and pro boxers alike. It's teaching by example, and it's not shadow-boxing. Laugh if you want, but don't take your eye off his right.

"I'm in the same shape I was in 1948 when I should have fought for the title," says the man who was the No. 3 heavyweight contender back then. "These guys think they can come in and blow me out, and when they can't do it, they get upset sometimes."

Chaney, who has developed a long line of thoroughbreds as head coach at the St. Rita gym on North Arsenal Avenue and now the PAL Club on East Washington Street, is what they call a local boxing legend. He's the stuff human-interest stories are made of—an ageless black wizard from Commerce, Georgia, who left home 40 years ago in quest of glory and ended up in Indianapolis as a police sergeant and a father figure to later generations of poor kids.

"We don't just teach boxing here," he says, jabbing his large, veiny hands into the cigar cloud formed by a steady blaze of words. "We build character. We teach kids how to face life."

Rangy and very dark, with deep-set eyes above smooth prominent cheekbones and close-cropped hair lightly salted with gray, Chaney looks every bit as capable as he says he is. He even lapses into a boxing stance—left foot forward, hands revolving at chest level—as he speaks. He's wearing hard-soled shoes with his dark blue sweatsuit, but he still gives impromptu rope-jumping and circling-and-jabbing demonstrations around the gym.

Past, present, and future flow and churn together when Chaney is around. Over here, he is patiently instructing a sub-teenage kid on the proper attack of the big bag. Over there, he playfully squares off with a young pro, or an assistant coach who also "fought everybody" in his day.

Always, Chaney remembers when he was No. 3 and, in his opinion, was robbed by the system of a chance to fight for the title vacated by the retirement of Joe Louis.

His only world title has come as a trainer; his protégé Marvin Johnson held the World Boxing Association crown for a while. But he addresses everybody who walks through the door of the PAL Club as "Champ" or "Champion."

"Everybody can be a champion if he wants to be. . . . There are no born athletes. You're born just a person hoping to go to hell. Anything you are is what you put into it."

In the gray light of early evening, in front of the wall of mirrors, Billy "Fireball" Bradley is bouncing and backpedaling, exhaling through his teeth with each violent thrust of his taped hands.

Pheet! Pheet! Pheet!

Then he moves to the big bag, a decayed leather cushion held together in the middle by duct tape. His thick back rolling constantly downward, his blunt face beaded with sweat, Fireball Bradley lays into the lazily swinging bag as he would tear it off its chain. Each blow is accompanied by a sharp grunt, kind of an amplified moan of hurt and desire.

Fireball Bradley is going to fight on ESPN next Thursday at Atlantic City. He's been training eight hours a day. Time is one thing he has plenty of.

"I haven't worked in about a year," he says, smiling. "It's rough, trying to train and eat. I have to make my living with these, and that's shaky."

He displays his hands, gloved in cracked leather, and resumes his assault on the rotting punching bag with the familiar label: "Everlast, Choice of Champions."

Catching Time in the Pocket

Baseball is born and dies and is reborn along with nature, spring and fall and spring again, year after year.

When nature's a little slow getting started, baseball shakes it awake and prods it along, sending kids out to swing and catch in the March rawness of early April, when bat meeting ball and ball meeting mitt feel like a fistful of tacks.

Then, when winter's waiting with its bony arms folded, throwing its shadow over home plate and penetrating windbreakers in the bleachers, baseball laughs its way through the last licks and makes the legends that outlive the coming darkness.

Baseball is both praised and condemned as the game in which time stands still. But while it's true each contest runs free of 45-second clocks and two-minute drills, baseball is the game most respectful of time in its larger, circular meaning.

Even with all the assaults on its integrity perpetrated during my generation—the indoor stadiums, the nocturnal World Series, the overextended season, the use of television gimmicks to fill in the "dead" spots—baseball continues to arrive when hope springs, leave when life falls, and rush nothing in between.

Like all established religions, baseball is grounded not only in nature, but in tradition. No more convincing display of the strength of that tradition can be found than in the willingness of a 20-year-old man, in the late twentieth century, to go through his days with a wad of tobacco in his cheek.

The rituals of other major sports—the high-fives, the end-zone dances—change as often as the sponsors' commercials.

Baseball has its fads as well, but even its most jaded superstars agree that the pitcher always gets the ball from the third baseman after it goes around the infield. The superstars, having chosen a sport where everybody gets a turn, have no choice but to know their place.

Just as yoga without chants and incense would be mere stretching, baseball without its countless ceremonial details would be—I don't know—slow-motion football.

A few years ago, I wrote about an inner-city youth baseball team formed by a fellow who liked the Los Angeles Dodgers as much as he liked kids. He recruited high school varsity players and drilled them in the skills needed to win; but he had other requirements as well.

He kept The Book every game, with every hit, error, and stolen base accounted for. He made sure his on-deck hitter was in the on-deck circle. And when his pitcher got on base, whatever the weather, he had somebody run the Dodger-blue jacket out to him, as they did when the manager was young. Baseball is the rites of spring.

Perhaps baseball's supreme charm is that its charm cannot be explained. Any baseball believer suffering the fuming futility of a debate over the relative appeal of the major sports knows the only antidote for his distress.

He can let his mind withdraw from the argument and float away—in my case, to his front stoop, where he sits in tender spring sunlight rubbing neat's-foot oil into the darkening hide of a Rawlings Dale Murphy autograph model he has bought for his son.

The glove smells both fresh and funky, like a wet animal. It is a little stiff yet, for all the lubricant and the pounding. It won't ripen and conform uniquely to the small hand for a good while, maybe several seasons. It would not be hurried even if there were a desire to hurry it, and there is not.

One in a Thousand

That's a nasty, no-good little rat, that baseball.

It comes at you at 80-some miles an hour when you're batting and 100-some when you're fielding—hissing and hopping and hungry for a crack at your thumbs and your shins and your jaw.

Hit it? Catch it? Only if you get paid what Dave Winfield makes, not a penny less. It just may be the meanest single element in all of sports, that thing.

When you see a kid who takes it on, who stands up to an inside fastball and spanks it into the sky, who swoops down upon a vicious grounder and reduces it to a smooth double play, you more than appreciate it.

You feel as though the world has been set to music.

That's what keeps Bill Warren doing what he's been doing all these years—the joy of baseball, and the hope that this or that teenager might make it something more than a childhood interlude.

William H. Warren, former Indianapolis Indians director of player personnel, former Cincinnati Reds scout, unofficial mentor to many major leaguers, man of many careers and activities, counts as his first love his present part-time scouting work.

As "recommending scout" for Indiana, a kind of free-lance stringer who reports to the St. Louis Cardinals, Warren has three basic jobs: he evaluates local talent, he sharpens that talent through a series of summer instructional clinics, and he tells a lot of good athletes they're not good enough.

"It's very cruel, very difficult, very heartbreaking. The hard part is telling 'em. Their life, their dream—you almost shatter it before they get on the field, by telling 'em the truth."

The truth is, unless a youngster can run 60 yards in 7 seconds and 90 feet in 4 seconds, he has two strikes against him as far as the major leagues are concerned.

Warren and Don Dunker, the venerable youth league coach who codirects tryout clinics at Noblesville High School, may see a thousand good high school players before finding a major league prospect.

On a brilliant late afternoon, Warren is showing off an 18-year-old shortstop who might be that one in a thousand.

His name is Jeff Stout. He was Yorktown High School's most valuable baseball player last spring and graduated near the top of his class. He has college baseball scholarship offers. And he has a couple strikes against him—5 feet 7, 140 pounds.

But Bill Warren, after 40 years in baseball, has not yet said no to Jeff Stout. He stole 57 straight bases in high school. He runs faster than 90 percent of the players in the major leagues. And just watching him warm up makes the old scout smile. "The little things he does. He looks like a major leaguer."

Warren is inclined to recommend the Cardinals sign Stout, but he cautions Stout that he is a "marginal" big league prospect. Stout and his father, Mike, would be interested in a serious offer, but for now, they say, they are enjoying baseball and thinking about education.

Those are the business realities. While they are being sorted out, Warren takes pleasure in watching Stout and other swift, strong kids make the bats and gloves sing. He takes pride in hearing from them how much his instruction has improved their game. He knows that when word reaches the colleges that people such as he are interested in them, they get better scholarship offers. That takes the sting out of saying no.

"I know I've had success," says Warren, who fought that wicked baseball only as far as the semi-pro ranks himself, "because I've had hundreds and hundreds of parents get back to me. They love it. They respond."

Suddenly, he turns to watch as Jeff Stout backhands a grounder in the hole between short and third and fires to first for the out. Warren worked with him on that backhand.

"Could have had more vinegar on that throw," the scout says.

Lonesome Whistle

No. 10 is hot tonight. When he isn't burning the net with his jump shot, he's burning the calloused ears of Mark Andrews.

It is midway through the second half of a Tuesday C League game in venerable Dearborn Gym, that near-Eastside landmark. No. 10 has just gotten over a screaming fit that was set off when he failed to score and Andrews wouldn't call a foul on the defender.

Now, at the other end of the court, the referee has the audacity to blow the whistle on No. 10 himself. A 3-point play at that. The kid is apoplectic.

"*What!* All I did was *stand* there!"

Stringy hair flying, fists clenched, No. 10 stamps around in a circle, gaping with disbelief and outrage. As his shrieking trails off, his choice of words descends to a stream of profanities. But he doesn't look at the ref as he mutters them, and Andrews ignores him. Routine stuff.

A technical foul doesn't come all that easily in the rough-and-tumble class of basketball known as "industrial league." With no TV audience and only friends and relatives watching from the creaking balcony seats, Dearborn leaves the finer points of decorum to the high schools and colleges.

When the referees do crack down, it is because the panting, swearing combatants appear to be at flash point.

"You've got to keep control of the game," says Andrews, whose zebra-striped jersey is set off by the long red sleeves of a baseball undershirt. "When they get to pushing and shoving, you have to call a tech or they might start swinging."

Sometimes, they swing at the referee. Dearborn is rife with tales of refs who took punches in the heat of the action or found losing players waiting when they went to their cars. At $10 a game, it's no wonder good officials are hard to find.

"Some guys still think they can be the stars they were back in high school and college," says Steve Roe, who runs the leagues and helps with the officiating. "When they can't, they think the referee favors the other team."

A cozy echo chamber on the second floor of an aging hotel with aging men in its lobby, Dearborn is the answer to a lot of "Whatever happened to . . ." questions. Big names from the past in local basketball trade points with each other and share the scarred court with guys who barely know a pick from a puck.

The arrogance of the old stars is intimidating to referees, especially those who don't wear the certifying patches of high school or college athletic associations. But Andrews, for one, prefers to work with talent.

"It seems like the better players with the better-organized teams are easier to ref. They've been through high school and college ball (where you curse a referee at your peril), so they're not as likely to get upset."

Tuesday nights are the worst, he says: "A lot of hotheads."

Some say Dearborn is milder than it used to be. The new management certainly has tried to sweeten the atmosphere. The walls have a fresh coat of paint, the snack bar has been improved, and every winning team gets a pitcher of beer on the house. Fighters are automatically ejected and even verbal ugliness is supposed to be tolerated only up to a point.

All the same, industrial league is industrial league. There is a four-letter word, beginning with "s," that is used more here than in a Mel Brooks movie. There is enough righteous wrath to fuel another Inquisition.

"One, Zero, Red," Andrews calls out, raising his right arm and pointing his left toward No. 10.

"What?!"

Playing the Bad Hops

Sure, Bill Owens would love to have been there.

He knows some of those 75 old men who gathered in Cooperstown, New York, this week for a reunion of the Negro leagues.

He, too, remembers what it was like to play big-league-caliber baseball in the infamous-yet-fabulous days before the big leagues lifted the color barrier.

He played against the best, the dead giants who were installed in the Hall of Fame so many years late—Satchel Paige, Josh Gibson, James "Cool Papa" Bell. He heard it when it was new, the story that Cool Papa Bell could flip the wall switch and be in bed before the room got dark.

"That Bell, he really could run. Fastest man I ever saw. When I was playing shortstop, I'd have to come in middle-ways. I couldn't play my position and throw him out."

That was a long, long time ago. Bill Owens played from 1922 to 1933 for various teams in the Negro leagues, including the Detroit Stars, the Chicago American Giants, and the Indianapolis ABCs. He will be 90 in November. He had a stroke three years ago and walks with difficulty. His wife, Rogie, who is 78, is seriously ill.

Owens can't imagine how he'll ever get to Cooperstown, which now has a permanent exhibit honoring the old showcase for black baseball talent to which he is Indianapolis' resident link.

"I was reading about that this morning," he said. "That guy

[Samuel Hairston of the Indianapolis Clowns] said he cried every time it was brought up how they'd been bypassed."

Owens doesn't think much about baseball these days, and when he does, it is not with bitterness—even though he believes he could have played in the major leagues if he had been born later or born white.

"No, no, no, no. Do I feel bad because that [integration] didn't come along in my day? No, it's just one of those things that happened. I'm just tickled it came along when it did. We've always been struggling. It's a way of life. I don't have any hard feelings.

"See, I came up differently than some others. I grew up in a mixed neighborhood. A lot of my friends were white. It gave me a different attitude than other people who were not around whites."

Bill Owens grew up in Haughville on the Westside, the grandson of slaves and the son of a man who believed adolescent boys should be doing chores, not chasing balls. "We got a whipping every day for playing baseball," the son recalled. But with pain came gain.

Owens didn't get rich playing baseball, but he got paid when the owners were honest and had money. He traveled all over the eastern half of the United States, stayed in the "nicer colored hotels," sometimes played in front of crowds as big as the white teams drew, and often beat the major leaguers in exhibition games.

"The grounds weren't like they are today. You see a guy make an error and he says the ball flattened out on him. I'd catch flat ones and all in my day, if I'm not bragging."

If there's anything he would like to have back, Owens said, it is his decision to drop out of school when his father died. That was sixth grade, and he didn't return to finish elementary school until he was 38. On wits and experience, he has owned a tavern and a poolroom and otherwise supported his family since baseball without working for anybody else.

"The only thing I ever regretted in my life was that I didn't go to school. I love to express myself. I'd love to be a writer. I'd love to write a book about my life."

Mano a Mano

He had been around some, this young man in Jesus-length hair and faded jeans who was half-reclining in a nightclub chair and half-watching a couple of guys flailing at each other in a boxing ring.

He'd been an amateur boxer himself, a Golden Glover. He carried a neat little scar above his right eye as testimony. He'd also played some football, had been in his share of schoolyard fights, had ridden some motorcycles, and had drunk some beer in his time.

Going at another man up there in the lights above the crowd, he said, "was the biggest rush I ever had."

I tried to imagine what it would be like, taking whatever strength, speed, training, and chutzpah I had and testing them on a snorting, dancing fellow man whose consuming desire was to hurt my body.

George Plimpton climbed into the ring to feel it for himself. Norman Mailer was an amateur pug of sorts. Their writing, I suppose, has the authority only malicious leather can impose.

Fine for them. I've had enough worries interviewing hard-handed old-timers who'd give me shadow-boxing demonstrations and miscalculate their distance from my nose. As a writer, though, I do take comfort from the rich trove of boxing literature produced by men and women who did not go so far as to lace on gloves.

Boxing has to rank right up there with baseball as an inspiration for prose; which is remarkable, considering how different the two games are, at least in image.

Boxing is sweaty and smoky and sexy, baseball serene and clean and green. Boxing is waged up close and personal, while baseball keeps respectful distances. And boxing is strictly mano a mano; not a lot of little girls petition the courts to be Golden Gloves novices.

From a fundamentalist perspective, though not necessarily from my own, there is no sport as obviously sinful as boxing. Besides the violence at its heart, there's the alcohol and the cigars and the women in spike heels on the fringes. Ironically, the kid in the ring is counseled to avoid all the temptations, including Eve, so he may be at his best for one of the most sensuous public activities a man can indulge in.

The boxer, the man in the clearing, is the innocent party—especially when he comes from a tough neighborhood and is lucky enough to make it under the wise wing of a Champ Chaney or a Honey Boy Brown or one of the other ex–pug masters. If he's serious enough about the manly art, he may become so attuned to rules and rigors and pure-mindedness that he'd be a lamb in a wide-open street fight.

That's OK, though. One of the bruisers Muhammad Ali whipped in his prime said after the bout that he wished he could have gotten the champ out in the alley. We laughed. Who cared?

Boxers alone together, up there in front of the customers relaxing with their beers, give each other too much to be natural enemies. "You never see a sport where they shake hands more than boxing," the ex–Golden Glover alongside me observed.

Two of the fighters on the exhibition card we were watching were pals to begin with, and it showed. Their sparring was lively enough but seemed pretty tame, and they smiled and jived between rounds. Just playing, I assumed.

But when I walked up to one of them afterward, he wasn't the same laid-back joker I'd met before the fight. He was drenched with sweat. His eyes between the head pads were wide and fixed.

He nodded woodenly when I spoke, his white mouthpiece thrusting at me like a declamation.

"Hello, stranger," his silence said.

Us Sensible People

A heady bouquet of hot metal, tortured rubber, and untreated exhaust wafts over the pits of the Indianapolis Speedrome, where Joann Roberts struggles with the spare tire to a wrinkled white Chevy Nova.

Track noise, like a hundred refrigerators tumbling down stone steps, forces her to communicate at a shout. But the important information is in writing, beginning with "Jo" scripted on the front of her yellow T-shirt.

"Arnold," the driver's name, is lettered in blue above the Nova's glassless window. A blue "42" is hand painted on the crumpled door. And "D-L Service Center" is everywhere there's space to put it on the battered Chevy competing in the Speedrome's slambang stock class.

You don't need a scorecard to identify the team from D-L Service Center, and you don't have to be a mind reader to tell how they feel about the effort by city hall to shut down the Speedrome.

"Some people like to go drinking. Some like to go to their flashy parties," Joann yells into the roaring and scraping. "Us sensible people should be allowed to have some fun too."

Her bright smile, large-framed glasses, and pulled-back hair would seem to place Joann Roberts in a kindergarten classroom rather than in this man's world of black fingernails and purple language. But the petite wrench jockey is hardly the only variety here.

From her battle station next to the pit gate, she can look, a hundred yards east, where the feisty veteran Billy Arnold pokes under his racer's hood with arms thick as her waist.

To the west, she can see a bespectacled funeral director named Gary Grose preparing to take the wheel of his immaculate pro stocker, dubbed "The Undertaker."

Within shouting distance to the south there is Ray Godsey, his sharp, tanned face permanently alert, standing alongside a menacing white modified Camaro—officially called an Outlaw—with which he will win tens of thousands of dollars this year.

Throughout the classes—the bare-budget street stockers, the uppercrust pro stockers, the big-money Outlaws, and the USAC midgets—there is unanimity on one issue.

Speedrome folks believe the city has better things to do than to wage war on their track, particularly when management has tried so hard to satisfy complaining neighbors. Besides the thousands of dollars in structural improvements, the track has set its own maximum noise levels and has disqualified top drivers for exceeding them.

But the city's lawsuit, alleging the Southeastside fixture violates zoning regulations, lingers on. The Speedrome has fought back with petitions, claiming 4,000 signatures. Even some of the race cars bear bumper stickers alluding to Mayor William Hudnut and the sports cathedral he plans for Downtown: "Hudnut Can Have His Dome, Save the Speedrome."

The Speedrome will survive the legal threat, but it pervades the atmosphere in this spring of 1982 like fumes from burning oil. It clouds the hopes of Arnold Sosbe, who won $300 last season driving for D-L Service Center and wants to drive an Outlaw some day.

Sosbe would follow the tradition of Ray Godsey, who kicked the windows out of his '51 Ford and went racing 19 years ago after a traffic judge suspended his license to drive on the street.

The custom-tailored machine Godsey drives now may not match the thunder of an Indy car, but it is just as far removed from the grunt and clatter of that old Ford. Its grille covered by a Fiberglas apron that nearly scrapes the pavement, its rear end held down by a U-configuration of spoilers, the Outlaw sweeps the one-fifth-mile oval with a nasty tearing sound, like lions opening an antelope.

The Outlaw doesn't need a muffler on the dirt tracks where Godsey usually races. Installing one at the Speedrome hasn't kept him from challenging the qualifying record. Godsey tends to chuckle at rules changes.

Across the pit lane, Sosbe gazes at his Nova and Godsey's Camaro and worries about the rules outsiders might make. He may wrestle an Outlaw in dreams, but right now he just wants to be an auto mechanic with glasses who decides for himself how to spend his weekends.

"I guess it's the spirit of the place that means the most. Other people get high on booze. I get high in here."

In the cockpit. Behind the "42" and below the "Arnold."

Scoring in Silence

Bob Kovatch kneels in a semicircle of wet, heaving, numbered bodies, scrawling asterisks onto a miniature green chalkboard. His basketball team trails 15–14 at the first quarter break, and he's not at all pleased.

"When you set the screen, you must break fast. You're wide open! You're standing there watching!"

For all his irritation, he speaks into the tumult of the high school gymnasium at a volume more suited to the dinner table. His hands do the shouting—slapping a player on the knee to get his attention, placing his first two fingers of each hand near his eyes when he says "standing there watching."

Mike Johnson, No. 32, sucks from a plastic water bottle and nods at the bearded, bespectacled coach. Johnson has kept the team in the contest with his soaring offensive rebounds, but he knows he's missed chances to cut to the basket for easy points.

On the first possession of the second quarter, he brings the chalkboard diagram to life.

The play starts with Johnson and another forward shoulder to shoulder on the right side of the free throw lane. It climaxes with Johnson spinning away and taking a looping pass at the lower edge of the glass backboard. Two points.

As the bleachers erupt and the white-skirted cheerleaders bounce like pistons, Kovatch shoots an approving fist at the athlete loping by and returns to his seat—but only for the moment.

One of the privileges of coaching basketball at the Indiana School for the Deaf is an informal exemption from the statewide rule that says high school coaches must remain on the bench. Understanding referees usually allow Kovatch to pace the sidelines, knowing visual communication is the only kind he has while the ball is in play.

Some of the disadvantages the Orioles face against hearing teams are obvious, but there are innumerable subtle problems.

Being forced to turn and see what's going on, deprived of the help of a shout or a squeaking shoe, costs a lot of half-seconds that take their toll in this blink-and-he's-gone sport.

Falling behind is dangerous, because the opponent may then draw you into a man-to-man defense, which puts your back to much of the action.

And what becomes of the home court edge when you cannot hear the cheering?

Well, on this recent Friday night, the home court edge cuts mighty deep.

Beaten on the road in overtime three weeks earlier by their rivals from Lutheran High School, the Orioles take revenge on their own floor by a deceivingly close score of 69–58. Johnson, with 20 points and 17 rebounds, and Francisco Villot, the other forward, with 22 and 14, lead the way as usual.

The victory is the ninth of the year against five losses for the quick, disciplined Orioles, who seek their first winning season in more than a decade. They've lost twice by just two points, including the title game of the Central States Deaf Schools tournament last December in Wisconsin.

The young coach has a feeling success will not wait. Thoroughbreds like Johnson and Villot, who are seniors, do not come around often to schools of any size. Deaf School's enrollment is only 250 and that number is swollen by the rubella epidemic of 20 years ago; it figures to shrink in the future.

But the future is far away. From the moment the cheerleaders sign their recitation of the national anthem—under the direction of Mary Kovatch, the coach's wife—tonight is one to savor.

When it's over, Kovatch flips the light switch in the jubilant locker room as a signal to the troops to gather around him.

"Now you can see why I was so upset we lost to Lutheran three weeks ago," he tells them, orchestrating his fingers, palms, and fists. "We did not play an ISD [Indiana School for the Deaf] game then. . . . Tonight we proved we are a better team."

The players disperse, grinning, clapping, and signing. Villot seizes Johnson in a headlock. Somebody else, soaked and naked, warily circles a teammate who is whipcracking a towel.

On the large blackboard at the front of the room, an old shout is raised in foot-high letters, "KILL WISC DEAF."

Guarded Dreams

The Indiana Pacers call it their Walter Mitty Camp, conjuring visions of nearsighted file clerks with two-handed dribbles and crazy dreams.

The Walter Mitty Camp, after the inept, wimpish literary character who made all the rest of us losers feel dignified.

The idea is fine as far as it goes. Few of the 30 men invited to the Pacers' special free-agent tryouts this week had a prayer of becoming Indiana Pacers.

But when the whistle blew and the sneakers started squeaking, there was an acute shortage of things to laugh at.

When a man 6 feet, 7 inches tall and 200 pounds comes thundering down the middle of the court, sails up over the basket, and then gets knocked on his behind by the dude playing defense, it's real.

Walter Mitty, you best be gone from here, boy.

"The NBA is unbelievably competitive," said George Irvine, the new Pacers coach. "When you get guys who were pretty good college players paying their way to get a tryout, you realize how competitive it is."

Guys like Ricky Hall, Purdue University's cobra-quick guard, who is small by pro standards but a blockhouse next to the man on the street.

And David "Poncho" Wright, a 6-foot-6 pogo stick from the University of Louisville who was on national television as much as the Culligan man.

And Lloyd Batts.

Lloyd Batts was easy to spot at the Walter Mitty Camp. In contrast to the skull cuts favored by young black athletes, his hair was long and loose, a kind of cross between the Michael Jackson slick look and the puffy Afro they used to wear in the old American Basketball Association.

A graduate of the University of Cincinnati, Batts was in the ABA from 1974 to 1976. He and Irvine were teammates on the old Virginia Squires. That seems like a long time ago, the days of the red-white-and-blue ball and soaring Connie Hawkins and big bad Reggie Harding. And it was.

Lloyd Batts is 33 years old. His pro career in this country ended, for all intents and purposes, when he broke his ankle during his rookie season in the ABA. He hung on a couple of years, then went to Europe and played eight years before returning to his alma mater, Gage Park High School in Chicago, as a teacher and varsity basketball coach. The last time he was in pro tryout camp was "four or five years ago." He came to this one because Irvine gave him a phone call, and he has no Walter Mitty illusions.

"I bought a home in Chicago and I'm going to try to settle there—unless something develops," said the lean, muscular man with the broad, alert, child's face. "If I get a year with Indiana, fine. If I get two years, fine. If I don't, nothing's lost."

As it turned out, Batts did not make the cut. But neither did a lot of better-known players 10 years his junior. While he insisted he did not consider his age a disadvantage (the Pacer brass certainly did), Batts did concede that a pro scrimmage can be a path to truth.

"You find out," he said, "if it's your time to stop."

He was asked how important basketball has been in his life.

"If it wasn't for basketball, I'd be maybe dead, maybe in a gang, maybe in jail. Basketball gave me a chance to go to college; it made everything possible. Being a black, a minority, one of the hardest things to do is come from a bad situation to a good situation and then keep the good situation going."

By that, he means using basketball after the glamour is gone. Europe, where he played well but tired of the rootlessness, was one way. The coaching and teaching are the next step.

"If I don't make this, we start work right after Labor Day. That's what this is, just a job. I like to work with kids, anyway. I'd like to give back some of what I got."

What he got this week was one more time in a pro basketball uniform. Nothing crazy about a three-hour drive for that.

No Place to Play

The garage is still standing, and so is the stone wall where we used to take the ball out of bounds. The alley is so narrow, so rocky, it's hard to believe we played even half-court games there.

But it was The Spot for a few years, so jammed with serious players some days that the squirts had to hustle over directly from school if they wanted to get in without calling "winners" four games ahead.

I'm pretty sure that's how it went, anyway. I don't remember Southside basketball with precision any more, but that place is the first one I think of.

I learned to shoot a jump shot there. I learned about the jungle ethic teenagers sooner or later have to deal with. I played with a guy who would become the first person I knew to die in Vietnam.

The backboard is gone now. The garage door bears a "No Parking" sign, which would have been a joke back then. The stone wall is black with graffiti and jagged at the ends.

A lot of change, for better and worse, has happened on the Southside since the early 1960s. The places I played basketball, in the old neighborhoods a mile or so south of Monument Circle, did not make the cut.

It seemed a natural to revisit those alleys and asphalt lots on this glorious occasion, tourney time, 1990, when a Southside Indianapolis school was appearing in the state boys' basketball finals for the first time since 1961.

I was 12 in 1961. The miraculous Tom and Dick VanArsdale

were starring for Emmerich Manual High School, and the deseg-regation order that would give Southport High School its heroes in 1990 wasn't even a gleam in the judge's eye.

It was the year the Berlin Wall and the first ICBM went up. We played to 24 by twos, win by four, and nothing in the world hurt like losing one of those games.

Return there now, and the losses pile up.

From the alley off South East Street, I moved on to the schoolyard where I once lost a tooth in a redneck basketball scuf-fle.

My only company was a calm squirrel that stared from atop a brick wall where the goal used to be.

Then I tried the garage off Shelby Street, where my once–best friend had stroked a sweet fadeaway jump shot that left me flushed with envy. The weeds were still there, the garage was not. The twisting alley was like a back street in Manila, barely wide enough for a car, strewn with trash and a wrecked grocery cart.

I tried the parking lot behind the fire station, where we had played into the night under lights that blinded as much as they helped. The basket was down; a tall security fence was up.

There were lots of security fences, lots of "Keep Out" signs. Nobody was playing buckets in any of the places where we had scraped and cursed and pretended we might yet wear a uniform.

That's my Southside, at the height of basketball season, scene of a sadness strictly personal. But there's nostalgia to be shared, too. After the alleys, I had the Madison Avenue Flower Shop on my list.

Melvin Nordholt's family business was in its second century and third generation when he put up the red-and-white stream-ers in 1961, honoring the school next door. He and his son, Steve, were at Butler (now Hinkle) Fieldhouse when the Manual Redskins lost in overtime to Kokomo.

Melvin still has the March 24, 1961, edition of the school newspaper, with its photo of the disconsolate burr-headed Van-

Arsdales accepting the state's first dual Trester Award for mental attitude. It's not something he digs up often. The past doesn't much occupy him.

"We couldn't touch the ball in the last minute and a half without getting a foul called on us," Melvin said. "But that won't change the final score."

The Madison Avenue Flower Shop was my next-to-last stop. The last was an asphalt court off McCarty Street to which I used to walk a mile with my basketball, sometimes in the rain. Now, the court is a hole with a security fence around it and a power shovel inside it, building and burying.

Duel in the Sun

Kenny Nash has been dunking all day on the killin' hot asphalt of Tarkington Park.

Quick-dippers. Reverse jams. And now, the helicopter power slam.

His scarlet shirt clinging to him like maroon paint, he leaps toward the basket with his left arm extended horizontally, serving as a rudder, and scoops the ball with his right hand from knee level to the netting in a faultless, in-yo'-face arc.

FOOM!

Back in his high school playing days, Kenny Nash would have brought the Arsenal Technical High School fieldhouse to its feet with this aerial show. He has a tougher audience here at 39th and Meridian streets.

For one thing, just about everybody watching is a ballplayer, whether he's making the scene in high-top Adidas and wristbands, like Nash, or in sloppy canvas sneakers and old dress pants cut off at the knees.

Besides, it's the middle of the afternoon, 90 degrees, and a good share of the enthusiasm for ball has been sweated away. The place will be packed come evening, when the punishing sun diminishes to nothing more than a shooter's hazard at the west basket, and dudes will have to call "winners" five games ahead.

Right now, there aren't more than a dozen players hanging around under the two leaning goalposts or slouching in the merciful shade on either side of the court.

About the only thing that can hold their mild interest is

Kenny Nash and Will Beverly going one-on-one for $25.

The game is supposed to settle a dispute that began in a tournament last week, when Will was player-coach and Kenny got less playing time than he thought he should have. Nothing will stop the jawin' except a duel in the sun.

The grudge match starts out fine, with Nash swooping in for dunks and burly Will using his hip to keep Kenny's long arms out of the way of his layups and five-footers.

Back and forth they go, scraping their soles on the sandpaper pavement and clawing for rebounds, hissing expletives when their long shots refuse to drop and bouncing with new vigor when the short ones fill the net.

"Take it to the hoop!" the partisans yell. "Don't be takin' no jumpers!"

There's nothing like summer heat, bent rims, and gray dust to take the edge off a mano-a-mano showdown. It isn't long before Nash and Beverly are heaving and panting like a couple of boxers in the 14th round who've been transformed by fatigue from enemies to dancing partners.

Darrell Davis, one of the regulars, shakes his head as the two men pound after a loose ball. "They tired and hot, boy! It's a mother out there!"

The score is tied something like 12 to 12 when Nash and Bevery cut it off. Beverly drags his muscular body like so much dead weight to the water fountain. Nash takes his shirt in his teeth and stands for several minutes next to the court, bent double.

"I play around town a lot, and these guys don't," big Will says a few minutes later as he sprawls on the grass. "I play with the college guys, the pros, the has-beens, the never-weres, the will-bes, and the never-will-bes. Every time I come around here they feel threatened. It's a challenge to them."

Maybe so. Nash has no time to argue about it. He's already back on the court. And as usual, he's got everybody's attention. Even Will, who is careful not to sound too impressed when he talks about Kenny Nash, wants to see the dunk show.

With the court cleared, Darrell Davis holds the ball under the basket at about the height of the letters ATTUCKS on his green jersey, waiting for Nash to start his charge from the left sideline.

Nash nods, bends slightly, turns in an easy semicircle, then breaks into a dead run that takes him across the free throw line at a sharp angle.

When he's within about 10 feet of the hoop, Darrell carefully lofts the ball to a height of about 11 feet, where it hovers for an instant, like a just-wounded duck. The eyes of all the brothers are on that grimy ball and Kenny Nash, coming like an express train in red shorts.

Helpless and indifferent, the big sphere hangs above the ragged net as the athlete's bulging calf muscles lift him up and over it. For a sliver of a second, he seems to study it, wide-eyed, biting his lower lip, caressing the ball with long brown pianist's fingers and lingering in midair until that sweet moment, that godlike explosion of ecstasy, when he shoves it down, down, down to basketball hell in a clean, ruthless, rim-rattling jam.

Uuuuuuuhhhhnnn!

A couple of guys applaud. Somebody lets out a war whoop from across the street. Darrell Davis jabs his fist in the air and laughs.

Kenny Nash walks over to Will Beverly on the ground and proffers his hand.

"Let's call it a draw," he says.

"Yeah," Will says.

They shake — just four fingers hooking at the first knuckle, uptown style. Then they're back out in that baking sun, where dudes are getting up sides for a full court game.

Giving Thanks

Older than the oldest fan and new as a pure spring evening, the sounds of baseball smack and rub against each other in the pregame languor of Bush Stadium.

Fans chatter about earned-run averages and won-lost records to the dull, stony beat of a pepper game down on the field.

A gray-haired usher points to a young Indianapolis Indians outfielder and proclaims "That's a hell of a good little ballplayer and don't you think he ain't."

The P.A. system barks out an unnoticed string of pop recordings and finally, a live voice that reminds fans to "have your pencils and souvenir programs ready for tonight's starting lineups."

Above it all, sharp and rich as a baritone saxophone, blasting from one end of the horseshoe stands to the other is the sound of Noel Douglas.

"COAL BEER! ICE-COAL BEER!"

For the last 25 seasons, going back to the days when they called the place Victory Field, it's been like the crack of bat against ball—an essential sound, and a noise whose maker is gone before it reaches any ears.

Taking time for a "Thank you, sir" at every stop, Noel Douglas covers more ground hustling beer than vendors carrying a third of his 56 years. He'll sell a tray of 20 dripping 20-ounce paper cups of Stroh's at $1.75 apiece before the first pitch is thrown in this sparsely attended weeknight game. On a good night, he says, he'll work his 15 percent commission for $100.

It looks like a struggle. A small man with a dark, solemn face,

"Doug" Douglas lurches along at a severe backward angle to counterbalance the load bouncing off his right thigh. Beer and condensation soak the blue change apron, the candy-striped tunic, the sheaf of currency tucked between his right hand and the tray. Sweat marks off the gray hairline below his white paper cap.

"I like baseball better than any other sport," Douglas says. "But when I get to workin', I like to take care of the customers. I don't like to bring anything back. I like to sell out."

Ask him if it's harder, now that he's no longer young, and he replies, "I can't tell any difference. I had a kid, 23, tell me 'I don't think I can go like you.' "

A native of Tennessee, Douglas started vending at Griffith Stadium, home of the old Washington Senators, in 1956, when he was stationed near there in the Army.

In 1958, the same year he came to Victory Field, he started selling souvenirs and newspapers at the 500-Mile Race. He still does that and still vends at Market Square Arena, the Indiana State Fairgrounds, the Speedrome—anywhere there's a sporting event, concert, or other festive occasion that draws a crowd.

He also travels around the country occasionally, selling souvenirs at rock concerts. He was following the Elvis Presley tour in 1977 when it was cut short by the singer's death, and enterprisingly headed for Memphis, where he and his buddies hawked their 3,000 leftover Elvis T-shirts at the funeral.

In addition to all the vending, Douglas holds a full-time job in the boiler room at Fort Benjamin Harrison, from which he plans to retire six months from now at the end of 1983.

"What do I do for pleasure? This is pleasure to me. I'll be at the track Sunday, selling programs."

Besides sheer hustle, Douglas has built his career on a keen sense of human relations. If the man at the top row has been waiting longer than the guy two feet away, go to the top; usually, the other guy will hang on. If the row wants four beers and you've just got two, give them two and wait to collect until you get back with a new tray. "I've never had nobody walk out on me yet."

Above all, he says, no matter how wet and weary you get, "Thank that man as much for a quarter as you would for a million dollars."

Get close enough to listen, and you'll hear it every time. "Thank you, sir," sure and sharp as "COAL BEER!"

Send in the Clowns

Dubois, Ind. — The vans are still warm from the eight-hour drive from Memphis. The Indianapolis Clowns are two players short on the roster, three runs behind the Jasper Reds, and four innings away from supper. They are playing baseball for money in front of a dozen people in a southern Indiana town that would fit inside the Astrodome, water tower and all.

This is a job for Sal Tombasco, alias Andre the Clown, alias Rocco, alias Captain Ahab Rocco.

The second baseman and part owner of the "Comedy Kings of Baseball" trots out to the third base line wearing an umbrella hat and Care Bears life preserver over his flowered shirt and shorts. With him is Susan Jensen, alias Sunny the Clown, blonde hair framing her red-and-white painted face.

They pretend to row a boat, using bats as oars. He pretends to be saved from drowning, spitting water when she pumps his arm. She removes his left shoe and pretends to faint.

"That's the same spike Hank Aaron wore in 1952 on the Clowns," Al Tobin, the general manager, croons over the public address system. "Geez, does that stink!"

The smattering of laughs comes mostly from the dugout of the Jasper Reds, the local semi-pro team that hosts the traveling Clowns every summer. The Reds know the elfin, indomitable Sal Tombasco well enough to needle him, and they know a trouper when they see one.

"I can't really clown if there's no crowd," Sal complains during the break. "I like to do a lot of person-to-person, get 'em up if there's a dull crowd. Let's face it, baseball's basically a dull game. You've got to really love it."

Clowning is indeed a labor of love at Dubois. But crowds range from several hundred to several thousand at many stops on the Clowns' 80-game tour of the eastern half of the United States, according to Tombasco. Every year, he says, things improve.

It's remarkable, the survival of the Clowns, a barnstorming anachronism born in the 1920s, best known as Hank Aaron's first employer and never based in Indianapolis. The old Negro Leagues tended to slap city names onto traveling teams arbitrarily, and the Clowns have kept theirs through many changes of address while outliving their parent by more than a generation.

More remarkable is the principal owner, Dave Clark of Corning, New York, who saved the team from extinction in 1983. A congenial blond fellow with a movie star's face, Clark has played organized baseball on crutches since he was 8. His braced, shrunken legs, the legacy of polio in infancy, are weights he drags to home plate. But spare your sympathy.

In the first inning, Clark leans over his crutches and snaps a perfect bunt up the third-base line. Toby Henrickson, who runs for him, is barely thrown out. In the sixth, Clark twists a solid single over shortstop.

"I'm not complaining: It's still a great life," he says, smiling and sweating after the Clowns' 8–1 loss. "Except for nights like tonight."

Promoted as an inspirational figure, inured to being a curiosity, Clark above all is a fierce competitor and a baseball head. He recruits the straight players who make up the bulk of the lineup—young guys who put in a year with the Clowns for expense money in hopes a major league scout will discover them. Sometimes it happens.

A golden opportunity will come July 5, in the Hubert Humphrey Metrodome in Minneapolis. Clark, down to a roster of 10 players, worries that the Clowns may not be ready. Sal Tombasco, alias Andre/Rocco, promises to break a leg, as they say in show biz.

"We'll have to have it together," he says. "You'll see us going nuts."

Reflections

Thinking on Foot

"Most good writers are walkers," said an excellent writer named Edward Hoagland, who never said no to a seductive generalization.

I don't habitually refer to myself as a writer because I've seen the best of writing, and I covet it, like a jeweler's apprentice holding a priceless watch. I've read writing that will levitate you from your chair, and it never comes with directions.

For most of us, that's how it is. Art is not to make, but, if we're lucky, to find. If the muse doesn't answer, try the library.

Long walks are a good way to go looking for the muse, or so I tell myself when I take walks through my neighborhood. It is fertile territory, starting out congenially urban with just enough loud mufflers among the baby strollers to give it an edge, and leading to a woods where prospectors still find pea-sized nuggets of solitude if they strike out early enough in the morning.

I used to prefer walking very late at night, steering clear of the woods, where I might stumble over roots or couples, and sticking to the sidewalk like a lighted shoreline.

But the sidewalk became treacherous. Somebody had taken to pulling up alongside nighttime walkers in a car and firing rocks at them. I was one of the victims, bloodied, disillusioned, grateful he hadn't aimed for my head, or if he had, had aimed poorly.

This is the urban edge, I realize. This makes the stars brighter and the mown grass sweeter away from the back yard, this feeling of having risked something for coins of the spirit. Everyone should walk alone late at night, even if he is inspired to thoughts no finer than the NBA playoffs and the vulnerability of his body. I do, but much less than before, and mostly in winter, when the thugs are less active and the stars in a black sky shine so hard you think you can all but hear them.

Early morning walks in spring pose a different set of problems to someone who wants to be open to the riches of isolation. Birdsong is as mad and massive as a rock concert at daybreak, but it already has competition from relentless automobiles and the huff and thump of serious exercise.

I was on a paved road that runs through my woods in the grayness of a recent morning when I heard what sounded like a public address system erupting from beyond a hill. It turned out to be the voices of two men in identical pastel shorts, out for a run.

Theirs was a wholesome and reasonable enough activity considering the range of possible human disturbance in a woods. But the effect on a walker—not a fitness walker but a watching and trying-to-be-lost walker—was like that of a fire engine.

To go and be quiet in a place still ruled by trees is an art and a craft, another real writer named Wendell Berry has said. I practice and practice, like a tone-deaf child who knows his parents spent their life savings on this violin, but I still can't identify trees with certitude much past the sycamore. I may as well walk fast, with pumping chicken-wing elbows; my thoughts won't nest here anyway. At least they have no roof to trap them.

Writers are walkers. At the edge of my woods, on the ground near a pond where a single mallard bobbed in sleep, I once spotted a pair of huge colorful beaded earrings, placed side by side like markers. One kind of writer would make splendid use of the duck; another kind would do wonders with the odd human clue. A walker who appreciates both would at least not waste the gifts.

Reverence

Approaching the celebrated Kanakaria mosaics through the hushed, palatial space of the Indianapolis Museum of Art was a lot like taking in the freak show along the carnival midway. There's the pitch—publicity, the signs, the automated video presentation. There's the long, tantalizing walk around the partitions and into the depths. There this mixture of dread and determination that, after all this buildup, these things have to be alive.

They are alive, of course. Beneath all the high-priced legal and aesthetic arguing, the point that Greek Orthodox religious leaders wished to make is that these two-foot-by-two-foot chunks from a sixth-century church ceiling are sources of intelligent energy. They speak.

Walking up to them, each in its own glass box, four flat faces formed from bits of marble, glass, and metal, I had this strange feeling I would hear them, not just spiritually but literally, and I and the rest of the curiosity-seekers crowding around might be eavesdropping on a conversation not meant for us.

It is not as if people who go to the art museum on a sunny Saturday morning, skipping the Persian Gulf victory parade on television, are a bunch of louts. But the sensation nagged at me all the same—I was gawking at objects venerated by millions of people long dead as if I'd paid a dollar to see the dog-faced boy.

Think of the circumstances that had brought us together:

• The wholesale destruction of religious art by government decree more than 1,000 years ago, a movement that spared the ceiling mosaic of a village church and thereby made it precious to the so-called art world as well as to the villagers.

• The invasion and plunder of Cyprus by the Turks in 1974, an event that saw the four fragments of the Kanakaria mosaic—faces of the boy Jesus, two apostles, and an archangel—ripped away and dumped into the black market.

• The soulless traffic in antiquities, which joined bizarre globe-trotting smugglers with Indianapolis entrepreneurs in a scheme to make $20 million off contraband objects of worship.

• The slow deliberations of judges, lawyers, and experts that had *The New York Times* itself waiting for their answer to a question: Can sacred artifacts that have held cultures together for centuries be bought and sold like yachts?

Jagged, dulled, and chipped, the four faces that looked back at me radiated a calm and a wholeness that mocked all the strife they had survived. They reminded me of some people I've known, who gained a little fame for one reason or another and found it funny because they actually deserved it. I pictured a shy writer at a penthouse party in honor of his best seller, trying not to betray his sense that the crumpled notes in his pockets will make a book that will outlast the best seller and all this grandeur.

Even if I were an art critic, I could not judge the Kanakaria mosaics because I could not separate them from all the baggage of a beauty that outlasts wars, politics, greed, and art theories.

I also felt a little guilty, belonging to the species that caused the forces that brought these holy relics to within walking distance of my house. But a little guilt is a good potion. I feel better for having gawked, and it didn't even cost me a buck. As a priceless experience ought to be, it was free.

Cheap Ticket to a Second Chance

You don't need a box seat to have a good view at Bush Stadium; but a box seat costs about as much as it costs to park your car at a Colts game or a Cougar concert, so once in a while, what the heck.

I hadn't sat that close in so long that I'd forgotten, or maybe was noticing for the first time, that these guys in numbered pajamas are kids.

"He really looks young," I said to my son as I turned from the skinny lefthanded pitcher warming up in front of us. "Well, he probably doesn't look young to you."

"Yeah," my son, the politician, answered. "He looks young."

I flipped to the pitcher's stats in the program. Age: 25. So now it seems I am at a point where 25 looks like 17.

I am also at a point where the average minor league ballplayer was born around the time I was in college.

He was born around the time of Newark and Detroit and Watts, our last previous round of urban convulsion, reawakened by the aftermath of the Rodney King verdict in Los Angeles.

As he struggles to develop the curve ball, or hit the curve ball, and win promotion to what the players call The Show, he vibrates with the promise, fear, and frustration my generation thought was all ours.

Realizing this more strongly than ever, I felt pleasure and regret in roughly equal measure as I watched the lefty warm up, my son alongside me with his glove at the ready.

On the one hand, the three of us represented the tragic cycle of history, its mistakes and disasters returning each season with new clothing and old, unlearned lessons.

On the other hand, we were riding this kind of roulette wheel of hope, buying into a game of succession that doesn't shut down in the worst of times. We were a little beaten up, even the youngest of us; but we were alive and not counting ourselves out of luck. Me, I wanted to save the world and forget L.A., and I wanted a foul ball.

It was a chilly night, jacket weather, but the beer man was busy. He made himself busy. He needed a 20-degree rise in the temperature to move his product, and he simulated it with his rap.

"Ain't nobody here got money?" he would shout out. "How can you sit in the front row when you ain't got no money?"

People bought $2.75 Millers from him at least partly out of appreciation for the way he made art of his work.

All this guy does is pour beer. All the guys on the field do is transfer a small hard object wrapped in leather from one arguably safe place to another. What we love is how they do it. It's creativity in pure form, unique to each performer but capable of touching anybody else who opens up.

We define ourselves when we play, and especially when we play at our work. When our work itself is play, we gather crowds who envy us to death and wish us eternal life.

The ballpark draws a chef's salad of people who share cigar-flavored breezes, low opinions of umpires, and simple desires—a hit right now, a win three hours from now, a foul ball once in a lifetime. The place is a spa with noise, a reliable restorative for some of us who grow weary of the so-called real world.

"Getting and spending, we lay waste our powers," Wordsworth said. Standing aside and watching kids, 25 years old or 10, whip baseballs from point to point to point, stitching a quilt of air—*smack! smack! smack!*—whose beauty is no sooner seen than gone, we hook back up to the source of power.

We got the win, by the way, on an error in the ninth. We'll take it. We were sure we'd get a foul ball too, and we didn't. Next time, it's got to happen.

Funeral Detail

Simon was far and away the hardiest of the goldfish. Burly and surly, he cruised around the porcelain castle and over the colored gravel like a whale shark, sucking up an occasional chip of fish food, doing absolutely nothing he didn't feel like doing.

Simon showed no apparent grief when his first bowlmate, Theodore, went belly-up. Nevertheless, the humans whose job it was to feed him and change his water deemed it cruel to leave Simon in solitary. They invested 69 cents in another pal, this one not solid orange like Simon and Theodore, but pinto-colored. Kind of reminded you of a Creamsicle, or a Tampa Bay Buccaneer. Ernie was his name.

Well, Ernie managed to increase the water displacement of the bowl without disturbing or exciting Simon—perceptibly, anyway. The pair swam in different directions and in the same direction, occasionally bumping. Ernie gaily flitting, Simon just scowling and gliding ahead, slowly, slowly.

Their lives seemed, if not festive, at least complete. Symmetrical. Living in a fishbowl, whatever its other trials, would not mean staring out longingly at a world in couples. Nuclear families prevailed on both sides of the glass.

Then Ernie cashed it in. He was found one morning floating sideways atop the water, one black-and-yellow target eye gazing upward, emotionless, but deceptively alert-looking. Simon was on the other side of the little porcelain castle, near the bottom, barely moving, but upright, cold and alive.

Like Theodore before him, pretty, painted Ernie received a

crude burial in some poorly traveled, quickly chosen patch of the backyard. This was after he had floated in a aluminum roasting pan on the back porch for a day awaiting a decision by the humans as to whether to tell their four-year-old son about the tragedy.

After enough visitors, including an insurance salesman, had viewed the remains, cowardice and good taste forced the decision. Ernie would be thrown into the ground (more civilized than flushing him down the can, the traditional, domestic burial-at-sea), and the boy would learn of his passing in the abstract.

So far, so good. Two loved ones lost, but no tears, no hard explaining and no empty fishbowl as long as there was Simon. Brooding, barrel-chested "Refrigerator" Simon, survivor of a nursery school show-and-tell and many months of human dependency. Bulwark between the household and petlessness.

What brought him down was an ailment known to fish owners as "ick." His own body was fouling his water somehow, and the morning when he would be found floating was inexorably coming.

When it did, the decision was made to involve Simon's youngest human next of kin in the great rite of passage. Simon was placed in a sturdy little cardboard gift box, and father and son carried fish and shovels to the side of the garage.

It was slow going. Rain had softened the ground, but tree roots grabbed at the shovels and persuaded the chilled mourners to dig less deep than they wished.

The son watched, interested and silent, as the father said, "Goodbye, fish"—a eulogy that seemed neither too much nor too little. Then the two scooped the pailful of dirt back into Big Simon's tiny grave and trudged back to the house. Mom, watching from the kitchen window, said they looked grim, as though they were returning from the cemetery. The son did not ask for another pet, but he will.

Keeping the Bounce

Everybody seems to associate basketball tournament time in Indiana with blizzards, but the spectacular death throes of our odd indoor sport are more likely to keep company with fresh new breezes, shining mud, and the eager yellow fingers of rebounding daffodils.

See, basketball around here is an outdoor sport, too. While a hardwood floor with glass backboards may form our sanctum sanctorum, come March we itch like starch-collared kids in church to take it outside. The sunlight pouring through those grid windows at Hinkle Fieldhouse (and soaking the skin roof of the Hoosier Dome) lends extra urgency to proceedings that have absolutely no need for it.

My bias is toward baseball; but the thing is, runny-nosed, frozen-fingered basketball can be played on asphalt long before the ground is dry enough for bats and gloves. In Indiana, we shovel snow off driveways to play basketball; we play when it's 104 degrees. But springtime, when we're juiced up on televised in-yo'-face do-or-die competition, is the season we really feel the bounce.

John Cheever wrote about the smell of rain that could fool you into thinking you were young again. Launching jump shots from a damp, sloped, cracked concrete court between wind gusts sets loose the most phantasmagorical delusions of youth, power, grace, nerve, fame, and physical appearance. The difference between what Alan Henderson can do and what a middle-aged fan of Alan Henderson can do — and it's only a matter of inches, after all — disappears in a spring-fed imagination.

In my time, in my head, I have bear-clawed rebounds with Bill Walton, swished two-handed pancake jumpers with Charlie Scott, driven and dished with Nate Archibald, stopped and popped with Isiah Thomas and rock-a-bye-reverse-dunked with Michael Jordan. I have taken a million shots that either won the game at the buzzer or, if they missed, resulted in fouls and second chances. This is liberation theology that demands no penance with your faith.

For many years, anyway. Alas, the knees and lungs eventually reach the point where no amount of fantasy can enable them to lift the moon over the mountain. Spring stops bringing out the kid in the ballplayer and brings out the ballplayer's kid, as the natural order would dictate.

When my college friends and I were cutting class to play basketball, we tried to envision a day in the far future when we would live without this fix. Like smoking cigarettes and staying single, it had to come to an end.

"I'll keep playing till I'm 35," one of the gym rats said, and it sounded extreme, obsessive.

Now I'm at the stage where 35 seems young, and I'm still dribbling away from the grownup chores, Peter Pan with a three-inch vertical leap.

Old guys who play basketball are a special breed. As a rule, they're not in it for fitness; the most artistic of them can use elbows to accomplish anything aerobics might do. They tend to prefer limp clothing in muddy colors to barber pole-striped leotards. They are remnant soul brothers, out there together in a small boat, past sight of the land of common sense.

At tournament time, when the latest orgy of high school and college hoops nears its exhaustion point, they check to see if they've still got a thirst.

Finding it, they check themselves and the balding Spalding for leaks, and spring forth.

Building Blocks

By the evidence available to me, my father was not handy.

He may have been handy at work, where he dealt gainfully for 30 years with machines I never saw.

At home, however, there were no machines, only appliances. There was no jigsaw, no power drill, no workshop. The only labor performed in the basement was the thawing of pipes. The garage was a facility for storage, not manufacturing. "Carpenter" was strictly a proper noun.

There's a hole on my memory wall where Americans are supposed to hang a picture of a broken bicycle wheel in a vise under fluorescent light. The only tools I recall were simple ones— hammer, hand saw, pliers, yellow-handled screwdrivers that were touted to be magnetic but weren't.

Men's work around our house was conservatively defined. The presiding man changed fuses, lit pilot lights, and plunged toilets. When the television went haywire or the porch buckled, the man of the house got on the phone to other men, and they came out and took care of it. With money from the work he did away from the house, the man of the house paid them.

This is not a criticism. Some people, including women, are handymen. Some people are philosophers.

The question is, do we have a choice?

Robert Pirsig, in *Zen and the Art of Motorcycle Maintenance*, argues persuasively that practical acumen can be acquired after birth and that lack of technical skill should not be excused as a sign of lofty intellect. Just because I can't pound a nail doesn't mean I'm a genius.

At the same time, my unhandiness is to some degree hereditary. My father had no feel for wiring or bricklaying, so he did not include those mysteries in his legacy bag, which was already stuffed with other treasures, such as baseball, religion, and joke telling.

Genetically, I cannot say I was impoverished. I had a teenage cousin who decked the roof of his house with a lighted display of Santa and reindeer, grand enough that the newspaper took a picture. One of my uncles would come home from work, eat supper, and go out and build a new garage. I could just as soon picture my dad and myself as Ferrante and Teicher.

I don't know that this lack of manual aptitude ever troubled my father. I coped by cultivating a protective disdain for tinkering, as an oyster artistically coats a swallowed piece of grit. This served me adequately until home ownership and parenthood when the pearl became, as in the John Steinbeck tale, a source of grief.

Ignorance of soffits and circuitry and plumbing can cost big, big money, unless you get lucky. I might have paid $200 to have a toilet fixed last month, had I not stumbled upon a $1.35 plug and randomly pulled something in the tank that stanched the water, a triumph representing me at my handiest.

I wish dollars were the only cost. No sum can cover the hurt an all-thumbs father feels when a small boy brings him an armload of scrap wood and asks him to build a tree house.

With sweat, swearing, outside help, and low standards, many father-son craft challenges of a less daunting nature will be met as the years go on. But true handiness, at this late hour, is an unlikely acquisition and an unlikely legacy.

The essayist Scott Russell Sanders wrote that he was hammering a new wall in his daughter's bedroom when he received news of his father's death. He paced several hours in a frantic daze, then went back to work, using his father's gifts of skill and tools to enact a kind of sacrament. I am aware we all have things of value to receive and pass along, yet I envy him that one.

Father's Day

When we were small enough to cruise the sidewalk along Prospect Street on tricycles, a highlight of our day would be that first glimpse of our father coming from the Fountain Square bus stop.

I remember his height, his wavy black hair, his gray work pants, and his easy, rocking gait. I remember my delight upon seeing him. But I don't remember doing much with him on those afternoons and evenings.

Oh, he played and talked with us. But mostly he did dad things. He went to work in the morning after drinking coffee, and he came home and read the paper and smoked cigarettes after eating supper. If we had been bad actors during the day, our mother might call upon him to interact with us in physically meaningful ways.

Dad was not much for family activities. He went to early Mass by himself, didn't attend school functions, never took us on a vacation, and never in his married life owned a car.

At the same time, he was a family man. He wouldn't miss work if he had to crawl there, he came straight home with his small paycheck, he wrestled with his kids and necked with his wife before their rolling eyes.

My mother died when I was eight years old, leaving five of us; and my dad received sincere advice to let an orphanage take his burdens. I had nightmares about being taken away by purse-lipped ladies in dark cars.

Dad kept the kids, of course; and while various substitute

mothers came and went over the years, he was both man and lady of the house as we understood those roles.

He wasn't great at it. He cooked, badly; cleaned, sort of; and left us kids to pull the wagon to the Laundromat.

He wasn't perfect and he often wasn't happy; but he was there. I would buy him presents for Mother's Day and Father's Day. He would insist the only gift he wanted was "having all of you here together," which I took to mean socks.

I've coached so many ball games and traveled so many miles with my son, it's strange to think how little my dad and I did together outside the house. A couple years after my mother died, he and I attended our first Indianapolis Indians game, keeping an eye out for the light towers of then–Victory Field as the bus heaved along 16th Street. He seemed nervous on these ventures, and it wasn't long before I was going by myself.

He was there when I got home, ready to regale me with baseball knowledge I'd already surpassed but hadn't the heart to argue with.

He was there when I got home from high school, though charitable strangers were paying my tuition.

He was there waiting when I packed my scholarships off to college, though he never saw the place and never asked much about it, from my first lonely bus ride to my solitary graduation.

He didn't keep the house all that well, but he kept it warm; and whenever the world got too fierce or I just got too scared, the old man was easy to find.

In my time, I have met men who were their children's best friends and men who boasted of how many welfare babies they'd made. I have seen fatherhood become an election issue. I've identified no standard against which to measure my father, and I don't use him as my own standard. I'm comfortable with his shortcomings and not particularly apologetic about my own.

I take pride that I am present; I know from him it's no small thing. I also realize, whenever my own son and daughter come running at the sight of my car, that the man who knew so much of lack and loss could have done a lot worse for himself.

Buried Future

Indianapolis may pause every February to remember its black history, but it doesn't have the time to revive that heritage and reconnect with it.

Like a forest that no longer feeds from the decay of its fallen leaves, the city grows upward and outward without regard for those who used to be essential to it: the old inner neighborhoods; the laborers and their jobs; the African-Americans who came north for colored work and hoped, at least for their grandchildren, for better work; the black communities that gave shelter and strength against racism even as they reflected it.

Some of their strength survives, but it has had its measure taken by the city.

Deindustrialization crippled the mobility of the black working class. Suburbanization, the great federal Marshall Plan for the middle class, lacerated African-American communities with freeways and bled them of resources. Downtown revitalization took root in the ruins of homes, schools, churches, corner stores, and jazz clubs—cultural loam that hosts foreign life it cannot nourish.

"The community is gone. Razed. Bulldozed," the black poet Mari Evans has written of her city. "Its striving, hopeful population scattered to the fringes of nowhere. Removed in the name of progress, to make way for a new population waiting, figuratively, on the drafting board. A new area, smart, new people—very few of whom look like those dispossessed."

The shadows of the city's rise of the 1980s obscured an enormous debt of hurt. The decade of sports stadiums, office towers, luxury hotels, cultural palaces, and tourism also saw Indianapolis lead the nation in the death rate of black infants. Though scores of millions of dollars from taxes and foundations subsidized glamour projects, money for expanded pre-and postnatal care for poor women came late and grudgingly.

The city tended to trade in IOUs (studies and proclamations) when it came to children and neighborhoods. Corporate subsidy (tax breaks, direct donations, eminent domain) was a cash deal.

As time passes, money must be applied like liquid nitrogen to make the privileged sector grow, because life has been sucked from the soil that used to be neighborhoods.

Inner-city schools have lost middle-class support and any claim they may have had upon the support of the poor who are left. Black males are more likely statistically to go to jail than to college.

Low-income housing is in critically short supply in a city that continues to raze neighborhoods and widen streets to accommodate the expansion plans of its wealthiest corporations.

Unheeded, the costs mount.

"There are 'quiet riots' in all of America's central cities," the National Commission on the Cities reported in 1989. "Unemployment, poverty, social disorganization, segregation, family disintegration, housing and school deterioration, and crime are worse now. The 'quiet riots' are not as alarming as the violent riots of 20 years ago, or as noticeable to outsiders. But they are even more destructive to human life."

Somehow, even in the dead and dying inner city, human life hangs on. For all the warlike stresses, for all the temptation to quick and deadly wealth, the norm remains home, school, church, and work.

For now, at least.

"They take the early bus," the Rev. Jesse Jackson says.

They wait for the rising city to wake up.

Maybe this decade.

Prayer for the Past

St. Meinrad, Ind.—We approached from the west, which is the wrong direction for feeling the full feudal grandeur of the religious edifices that overlook this tiny southern Indiana town and share its name.

The western way snakes up along the hillside behind a veil of trees, leaving none of our objective visible from a distance except the tops of the twin church spires.

From the east, the long view climbs and sweeps in wild luxury, like a hawk without a rival, joining the hummocky quilt of farmland and the leafy cameo village to the great crowning sandstone fortress that is St. Meinrad monastery, seminary and church.

Even at its most imperious angle, St. Meinrad could not match my memory, more ancient to my life span than the 136-year-old Benedictine monument is to New World history.

I had not remembered it from my childhood as larger or more majestic so much as older-looking and detached—a conjured castle in the clouds. Swing around a bend on Ind. 62, just past the gas station, and enter the Twilight Zone and the sixteenth century.

I knew enough not to trust that residual image. It dated to grade school and was ignorant of the Swiss and German heritage that enfolds St. Meinrad right along with the little wooden cottage churches that dot this part of Indiana.

As an adult, I was returning to this place not to travel back to the past, but to reach a vantage point from which the long connection between present and past would be discernible.

I wanted my wife and young son to see it because it traced, or at least located, roots of mine that are buried to them. For what it's worth, the middle-aged man they know spent one of the few out-of-town trips of his boyhood in this sanctuary.

That afternoon outing of 30 years ago was the idea of the parish priest, who thought I and/or a couple of my classmates might be clerical material. We toured the vaulted church, ate lunch in the dining hall, gaped as a shark of a priest cleared the rec room pool table, heard the absolute bells reset and reset the walking tempo.

Neither the vitality nor the peace of that community was sufficient to call me into its arms. The most lasting impressions it left were otherworldliness and intimidation, like something out of science fiction.

But what I yearn to believe now is that the reality and sanity of such a place, built as nothing today could be built and inhabited at a pace that never squanders a day, somehow stuck with me also.

St. Meinrad Archabbey is real and relevant, not so much because it has a gift shop and a volunteer fire department, but because it keeps its past present. In the three decades between my visits, rural Indiana communities were decaying from a blight of sameness spread by absentee interests for short-term profit. Every town on the way to St. Meinrad seems to have the same fast-food outlets as every other town its size; every patch of woods or water seems potential prey for the tourism industry.

This sounds like the sermon with which I bore my family in crabby midlife; but for all its futility, I sense it is right and that St. Meinrad is right.

Gazing at gray photographs of round-spectacled young priests in the tunneled white light of a century-old corridor, I felt as though I had delayed my return long enough to catch up with the slow, set movement of a faith community. I felt religious here, no more because the spires reach heavenward than because they are sunk into the hills.

We headed home with two pamphlets on the monastic life, purchased from the gift shop, a separate building to the east of St. Meinrad that affords that hawk's view of its splendor. "Are you getting ideas?" my wife asked, and she was not laughing.

Boys of War

If you ask about enough guys from the old neighborhood after 20 or 25 years, you'll get the bad news that isn't news.

So and so? No, he's not the one who's on the fire department. He didn't move to California. He didn't go to college or the auto plant or prison.

He got killed.

Yes, years ago. Fight in a bar, maybe. Or car accident. Or Vietnam.

Most often, that's what it is. Vietnam.

Count on a person my age from a working-class area to have a brother, cousin, friend, or acquaintance who didn't make it halfway to middle age because he got drafted or enlisted during the wrong decade.

Forever, he will be a kid in memory. A curled, yellowed comic book of random images and blotted pages.

A grimy pair of Converse All-Stars scuffing across an alley basketball court.

A stern boy's face under a drab green cap staring from an 8-by-10 on top of the television.

A bare-handed catch of a drive to centerfield, back to the plate, street shoes pounding the rocky playground, a rusty fence the only known danger, Vietnam not even a known word.

I heard the latest name just the other day. It annoyed me because I couldn't exactly remember who belonged to it. So many years and transitions have gone by since I saw any of these guys, the names have broken loose from the mental pictures. Softball without gloves and athletic shoes is a long time ago.

Was it the chubby, friendly kid with the pale-green eyes, or his older brother, the black-haired competitor who caught anything in the air but had trouble with grounders?

It's hard to comprehend either of them gone. Gone before manhood could get a foothold, before womanhood could share a fraction of its mysteries. Absorbed into the cultural memory of that part of America for which Vietnam does not conjure marches on campus and loss of faith, but marches down the trail and loss of sons.

At the height of the war from which our deferments temporarily shielded us, a college classmate said to me: "They can take that Vietnam and shove it up their ass." He, like I, was in the minority of students who came from neighborhoods that sent soldiers to Vietnam, and he knew somebody who had lost his lower jaw over there.

Shove it. I liked that. But it seemed too simple. I couldn't quite convince myself a generation could get away with not having a war. If we were going to have to bury our parents eventually, why should we not expect to bury some of our buddies now? Life has a price, I thought.

The truth was, luxury had the price. Student deferments, later the lottery, later the replacement of the draft by the volunteer military, have allowed some to sit and discuss the war while others go and die.

So many of them died in Vietnam, we expect to hear one of their names whenever we ask about any half-dozen guys from Mars Hill or Brightwood or Fountain Square. So many, we have to jog our memories. Freddie—didn't he get killed in Vietnam or something? Or was that his brother?

"We lost Davey in the Korean War," John Prine sang in a song about old people. "I still don't know what for. Don't matter anymore."

So with Vietnam, on the personal level. It happened, like a drought or an epidemic, and turned boys into memories. The undeclared Persian Gulf war likewise will add its flow to the cultural stream. At least one kid I know well stands a good chance of being in it, and I am working at remembering as many details about him as I can.

Out Back

In a conversation with my five-year-old son the other day, I happened to mention the word "alley."

"Addie?" he asked, looking perplexed.

"No, alley."

"Alley?"

"Yes, it's a little street that runs behind . . ."

My lord! It struck me that this boy, who knows all about streets and avenues and every manner of vehicle that rolls upon them, had never before heard of an alley.

Not that I should have been shocked. Though ours is by no means a suburban neighborhood, we are a couple miles from any residential area where alleys are common.

Alleys date to pre-television days, when lots were narrow and garages (which held one car behind double doors) were built behind houses rather than alongside.

Alleys are a central-city phenomenon, a working-class kids' habitat, and a privileged memory.

Nobody who grew up around a sodded cul-de-sac could appreciate the challenge of playing baseball on a diamond 10 feet wide, with a telephone pole for first base and a trash can lid for third. Pull it slightly foul, it lands in Mrs. Gibson's yard, she calls the police, game's over.

Alleys made us intimate, whether we liked it or not. They multiplied our number of immediate neighbors. If we got along with those on both sides of us, chances are there was somebody out back with whom coexistence took some work.

We learned from that. We learned a lot of things in the alley. We played every sport out there; we honed our bike-riding skills on minefields of broken glass; we practiced both block and cursive writing on those garage doors; we found out firsthand how nasty cigarettes can be.

Whether or not the lessons stuck, and regardless of their value, child-directed education thrived in the alley. It was a school of hard knocks, sometimes literally; but that was the price we paid for escaping parental supervision while barely leaving home.

It was dangerous. I remember. Glass. Rocks. Greasers cruising through from other neighborhoods. Cars. Especially cars.

A guy down the block from us ran jalopy races at the Speedrome. He used to test his cars in the alley, barreling through at what seemed like 90 miles an hour, showering us with gravel. How he got away with it and how we all survived it, I'll never know.

Physical safety was but one of many reasons parents preferred we stay out of the alley. They might as well have denied gravity. Only the weird kids, the ones who never got dirty, stayed in their backyards while the world roared by.

Often alleys functioned as both the locus of the action and the most convenient way to get to it. For example, our dirt-and-blacktop alley was fine for baseball and kickball, but lousy for basketball. So, we'd travel down our alley to Donahue's alley, which was nice and wide and concrete.

So popular was Donahue's alley for basketball, they said the VanArsdale twins, the stars who went on to Indiana University and the pros, used to play there. I can't vouch for that, but I remember that nobody was too cool to play alley ball in those days.

Even the city scoring champion, a guy named Ray, would join us for an occasional two-on-two or three-on-three on the "court" behind his house on Fletcher Avenue.

Ray had a curious idiosyncrasy—he wouldn't stand for swearing. We went along with that, thus demonstrating we could learn tolerance in the same classroom where we learned swearing.

Blessed Are They

I had this dream I ran into Jesus.

He was sitting in a White Castle, having coffee with three guys I recognized from the rescue mission.

Everybody else in the place noticed him too. Whenever he said something, ears cocked in his direction.

He didn't look so special, at least on the surface. He wore these limp, gross blue jeans and a plaid shirt full of paint stains over a dingy thermal undershirt. Duct tape held his sneakers together.

He did have shoulder-length hair and a pointy beard, but that wasn't what set him apart. It was his eyes. They gave off this soft glow that seemed to draw in all the other light in the joint and throw us into shadow.

When he walked over in my direction on his way for a refill, I spoke up before I knew I was thinking about it.

"Say," I said, "this might sound crazy, but aren't you, like, the Savior?"

"You win, bro'."

"Wow! No jive?"

"No jive."

"Jesus. So what are you doing here?"

"How much time you got?"

"I'll buy."

So I got his refill, plus a doughnut, and we sat.

"What happened was, I was hitchhiking yesterday and got dropped off by this trucker up on I-465," he said. "Real nice guy, always keeps a Bible on the seat. We jawed about it for 70-some miles. They're always impressed by my knowledge of the book.

"Anyway, he drops me at the North Meridian exit and I'm about to thumb my way Downtown when I get picked up. Suspicion of dope."

"Used to be vagrancy," I said. "You never had much luck with cops, as I recall."

"Or governors or preachers, for that matter. Anyway, I got hauled down to the lockup and strip-searched and kept overnight, and they dropped their charges this morning. No evidence. They sent my backpack with all my carpentry tools and folding money to the property room, and told me I'd probably have to sue them to get it back. Can they do that?"

"It's legal. What'll you do now?"

"Some good, I hope. I signed in at the mission and had some breakfast. Then I thought I'd take my last two bucks in change and buy these fellows some decent coffee. The coffee's terrible at the mission, but the prayers I like. The words hold up pretty well after all these years, if I do say so myself."

"Yeah," I said. "You're as popular as ever around here."

He froze me with those eyes.

"Popular? Me? Popular? You got to be nuts. What I said was, the words still hold up. Anybody who read the words has to know the world ain't ready for this old Jewish boy."

"But your name is plastered all over. You're about all people in this town talk about."

"That ain't me they're talking about. I wouldn't be caught dead in a million-dollar church when restaurants have got security guards watching their garbage. I sure wouldn't be riding around in some army tank blowing the bejeezus out of people. And if I tried to get in the White House, they'd shoot me."

"That's a drag," I said. "I mean, here you are, back just like you promised, and nobody knows it."

He smiled. "Shoot, lots of people know it. At least four or five know it just in the jail alone."

"That won't get it," I protested. "You need to spread the news. How about a miracle?"

He raised the coffee I'd bought him and finished it off. "This here's one," he said. "If I get my tools back so I can get work and free up a bed at the mission, that'll be two miracles. What do you want, man, heaven already?"

Cutting the Line

As they concluded the simple arrangements for disconnecting his late father's phone, the woman at the other end of the line surprised him.

"He was an excellent customer," she said.

Hey, that's one for the annals, he thought. A warm touch from Ma Bell. There are real human beings ushering us through these routines after all.

Of course, he couldn't prove the compliment was spontaneous. He chose to believe it was, largely because it was so hard-earned. Forty years of unfailing bill payments is not routine. He would have given it a kind word himself, had he been in that lady's place.

On occasions such as this, one is struck by the fact that basic day-to-day living builds monuments over time; that there is a great deal of history in ordinary lives, and in the ordinary objects that ease those lives along.

How can you disconnect a phone—your first phone—without feeling like a priest sealing a tomb?

In the case of the telephone, unlike that of the television, he was not old enough to remember when it wasn't there. He did remember, however, when the phone was a novelty, a homely little appliance of undetermined utility.

Melrose-XXXX was its name, later to be lengthened to Melrose X-XXXX, later to be shortened to 63X-XXXX as numbers consumed names.

The phone didn't age gracefully. It didn't age at all, but grew more garishly youthful with the passage of years and the elevation of Bell's marketing fever. Born in the 1940s as a black hunk of machinery, it went out as a sky-blue plastic toy, ludicrous in the dark old house it served.

How many thousands of times must that rotary dial have spun, in a place inhabited by as many as five teenagers at a time. How many weeks must have been totaled up, an hour or two at a crack, by high school friends in murmuring contact, adrift together in free space beyond the reach of adult authority and peer cruelty. How many forgotten intimacies must haunt its wires.

Intimacy did not always come easy. In the beginning, theirs was a party line. Anyone who subscribes to the Norman Rockwell ideal of American working class neighborhoods has not experienced a party line. The kids drove the lady on their line crazy, yet she managed to out-talk all of them combined. At its best, the relationship was one of tenuous coexistence; at its worst, there was shouting and slamming. Party lines tell us much more than McDonald's commercials about the nature of closeness in this society.

We all give that little jump when the phone rings in the middle of the night. He had hated the sound of telephones ever since his mother answered in the middle of a day and learned his aunt had mangled her hand in an assembly line accident. Such an eerie sensation it was for a child, witnessing sudden weeping without knowing its cause, hearing that terrible dialogue between an aproned woman and a faintly buzzing black handle.

The phone carried many sobs in its cargo of business and gossip and pizza orders and stumbling romance. It performed lots of vital work and wasted lots of time. In the end, each of its tasks weighed the same; the accumulation of life was all that permanently mattered. The last ambulance had been called, the last bill had been paid, and the noisy servant could rest; but not without a benediction to mark the passage. "Excellent," yes.

St. Pat's Survivors

"You missed a great chance," the disc jockey scolded as the last chords of "Louie, Louie" thump-bumped into oblivion. "Remember when the nuns wouldn't even let you play this?"

Remember they did, these not-quite-middle-aged members of the Classes of '61, '62 and '63, whom the DJ was trying to coax out onto the dance floor.

It was irresistible, the thought of this allegedly raunchy hit song assaulting the veiled ears of the stern and innocent Sisters of Providence. It was also, well, providential.

Here were the grown kids of St. Patrick School, most of whom had had no contact with each other for two decades, awkwardly trying on the idea of a class reunion. Furtively scanning the shamrock-shaped name tags to call up identities of old pals and old rivals and fourth-grade heart-throbs. Wondering how, when we'd gone so many directions, seen so much tragedy, reared high school–aged children of our own, a grade-school mixer would work.

But a few sparks was all it took. A little "Louie, Louie," a little Elvis, a team picture on display of burr-headed squirts pilloried in shoulder pads, a mention of those segregated spelldowns in which the girls could just about name their score. It all flared again, assuring us that nothing we've done since is important enough or dreary enough to extinguish those years.

"Remember . . . ?"

Sure do. St. Pat's on the near-Southside was the kind of place that claims the memory of millions of people of this and earlier

generations. Long since closed as a school, shrunken to a fraction
of its former size as a parish, it also typifies the sad exodus of
Catholics from the central city.

The neighborhood was world enough in the early '60s, when
John Glenn and Alan Shepard were breaching the Earth's atmosphere and a Catholic president was standing up to the atheistic
communists. Fountain Square was all the shopping center anyone could ask for, and rebellion was a tight skirt.

St. Pat's was a working-class, baby boom school, bulging with
brothers and sisters whose parents had every reason to see a wide-
open future. Though many of the kids did not go to college, it's
probably safe to say most of them did do better than their parents; they live a long way from the old neighborhood, anyway.

Nor would they recognize it today. Now a target of revitalization efforts, Fountain Square is a tattered study of grim survival.
Some of the big chain stores remain, but the movie theaters and
five-and-dimes and soda fountains of 20 years ago have largely
been displaced by second-hand stores and vacant land. Freeways,
government's gift to suburbia, have wiped away much of the community and isolated much of what's left.

The St. Patrick's complex is freakishly large for the handful of
parishioners who remain. The newest of its five buildings, the
convent—a two-story apartment house to accommodate the
cloistered teachers of a single school—was built during our time.
Imagine.

Nuns are fewer these days, and freer in their lifestyles. Once
concentrated in teaching and nursing, they are scattered over
many professions and doubtless are more worldly than those who
educated us.

None of our teachers made it to the reunion, as far as I know.
Some wrote, or called. Several are deceased.

It's too bad. I think they would have liked the party, booze
and loud music notwithstanding. For the most part, they were
rare people who really cared about other people's kids; and this
bunch, they would have agreed, turned out OK.

Living: Here's the Alternative

Writing, when it is done right, is a solitary grind, a kind of dying by millimeters.

Even in the newspaper business, with its imperatives of interviewing and shoulder-rubbing and general staying in touch, writing compromises human contact.

Insatiably, it milks people, their thoughts and their deepest feelings for material. Heartlessly, it forces the writer to keep after people for what he can use from them, and to live for the moments alone when he will dissipate his acquaintances and himself for the sake of the work.

Writing is the pusher. The writer is the junkie. He has little leisure to make friends. He cannot afford a full-size personality. People like him best when they read the stories that are his fix; but if they think they know him from the reading, they are kidding themselves. Driven by the writing, he doesn't know himself.

The consolation is in the thing of beauty, if he can make one. If the writing exhausts him and begrudges him the joy of honest living, it is not the worst addiction he could have. It lets him seize many people's hearts even if he can touch nobody's hand. Even when he reaches no one, he has a creation to console him.

Taking notes and tapping keys while the rest of the world struts past, all smiles and colors, the writer sadly tots up the special men and women he has come to sort-of-know. Exemplary people—bright, generous, original, spiritual, hilarious, brave. Hidden, for the most part, until he wandered away from the big house where news is made and found them in the fields, working.

His appreciation for good quiet people is an achievement great as anything he has written about them or for their causes. His sorrow is that his relationship with them is corrupted by his craft. Friendship asks nothing, and he always needs something— quotes, facts, tips, action to narrate, costumes to describe. Goods to fence for the pusher, to make the magic.

A couple years ago, I was at a funeral for one of those one-of-a-kind people — a fiddle player and songwriting genius named Lotus Dickey, who had reared eight children without a wife and had waited for his artistic recognition till old age without complaint.

The service was lengthy and beautiful, packed with people and music and tears. The party afterward lasted all night, as Lotus' hoedowns usually had. I declined an invitation to the fun. I realized it is not enough to be known and liked, which I was.

The person with the tape recorder and the space to fill cannot be a friend. He is the tourist in Amish country who makes sinful graven images with his camera despite his best intentions. He is an outsider forever if he never shoots or writes again.

"You're privileged," a friend told me when I remarked this at the funeral. It's special, in other words, to be the one who stands aside, observes and interprets and comes and goes. I can believe it when I read and reread my story about that exalting event, but I also remember how I considered writing nothing and letting the loveliness I had witnessed fill the world on its own.

For all his power to broadcast their names, the writer is humbled by the obscure heroes he celebrates. He's like a naturalist recording the dance of blue whales from the deck of a smelly old diesel tub, knowing there's some mysterious way these endangered treasures do not need his help or his admiration. He feels ridiculous and intrusive. But he will go ahead, alone, and make art of their sights and sounds, and take pride in how close he comes to their perfection.

DAN CARPENTER was a columnist for *The Indianapolis Star* for eleven years. As of 1992 he is assistant city editor. He has won numerous awards for his newspaper work and has published fiction and poetry.

DAVID HOPPE is senior program officer and resource center director for the Indiana Humanities Council. He edited *Where We Live: Essays About Indiana* (Bloomington: Indiana University Press, 1989).